Jodi Pawlusk

# mommy brain

## Discover the amazing power of the maternal brain

DEMETER

For my parents

Mommy brain: Discover the amazing power of the maternal brain
Jodi Pawluski, PhD

Demeter Press
PO Box 197
Coe Hill, Ontario
Canada
K0L 1P0
Tel: 289-383-0134
Email: info@demeterpress.org
Website: www.demeterpress.org

Demeter Press logo based on the sculpture "Demeter" by Maria-Luise Bodirsky www.keramik-atelier.bodirsky.de

Originally published in France in 2022 under the title Mommy Brain: quand le cerveau tombe enceinte by Larousse, Paris. English-language translation by the author.

Printed and Bound in Canada

Cover design: Jodi Pawluski, Zoé and Adam Charlier
Typesetting: Michelle Pirovich
Proof reading: Jena Woodhouse

Library and Archives Canada Cataloguing in Publication
Title: Mommy brain : discover the amazing power of the maternal brain / by Dr. Jodi Pawluski.
Names: Pawluski, Jodi, author.
Description: Includes bibliographical references.
Identifiers: Canadiana 20230496180 | ISBN 9781772584875 (softcover)
Subjects: LCSH: Mothers—Psychology. | LCSH: Motherhood—Psychological aspects.
Classification: LCC HQ759 .P39 2023 | DDC 155.6/463—dc23

 The publisher gratefully acknowledges the support of the Government of Canada

# Contents

# For you

In 2017, I co-authored a scientific review[1] with Prof. Joe Lonstein and Prof. Alison Fleming—two leaders in the field of maternal brain research—of the literature on how the brain changes with postpartum depression and anxiety. This review was published in a leading neuroscience journal and was widely accepted by the general public with popular press articles in many countries. It contributed to a growing narrative around the neurobiology of parenting and perinatal mental health: topics we have neglected for far too long.

From talking to journalists, clinicians and moms interested in our review, I was initially quite shocked to find out that simply knowing that the brain changes with motherhood was enough. That the knowledge that there are normal and important changes that take place in our brain to help us mother can come as relief.

There is a head on every pregnant woman and I think we need to remember that. It's not all about the "bump".

I also realized that moms, and those working with them, want to know what we know as neuroscientists studying the parental brain. This started my journey in sharing, with you, what I know and what my colleagues know, through my podcast *Mommy Brain Revisited*[2], interviews, blogs, and social media—and now with this book.

This book is a glimpse into how the brain changes with motherhood, fatherhood and parenting in general. I have focused on the brain changes in humans and less on the neurochemical changes or hormonal basis of these changes. There just wasn't enough room here and we still have much more research to do to figure out the details. For those interested, I would direct you to *The Parental Brain* by Michael Numan[3] which gives an overview of the neurochemistry of the parental brain based on years of research in animal models.

Beyond this, there is a need to understand the *amazing* role that the brain plays in motherhood. It doesn't go to mush. It reorganizes and shifts. It is also forced to cope with society's expectations of what it is to be a mother, which is a topic far beyond this book but one that needs to be pieced apart and redefined by us—mothers and parents.

# Part 1
# Mommy Brain—
# What is it anyway?

Chapter 1.

# Have you really lost your mind?

I'm sitting here thinking about everything I want to tell you about how amazing your brain is and what incredible things it does when you become a mother. I want to tell you everything I know and then some. There is so much that is amazing about being a mother, being a parent, but there are also so many things that are difficult about mothering, and it is probably one of the most challenging things that you will do in your lifetime. Being a mom will also last for most of your lifetime, but maybe don't think about that too much at the moment.

This is a book about your 'brain on kids' so let's take things in baby steps and start at the beginning with what we commonly talk about when we think about our brains and motherhood. (We will talk about fatherhood, but more on that later. For now, I'm going to focus on moms, because they are often expected—and this is still a reality in our society, let's face it,—to carry the brunt of parenting responsibilities—which, in my opinion, needs to change).

## I traded my brain in for kids

Mommy Brain. I'm sure you've already heard about this term or at least this phenomenon in magazines, books, blogs, and on social media... Emilie, a young mother and author of the blog Ninoute[4], sums it up well: "My neurons? My daughter has taken a ton of them (good for her)...

I still forget things. Don't worry, it's just during pregnancy, they said! Nonsense. It's actually quite worrying. Maybe I should get some help before I end up totally stupid.... I forget most things, but fortunately never the important ones. I have never forgotten to pick up my daughter from the nursery or to go to work. It's more about the little things in life.... But I'm not alone, my best friend just had a baby and she forgets things too."

And then there is this testimony from Josée Bournival, a Canadian TV host and mother of four. In a blog post entitled *Where did my brain go?*[5] (the title says it all!) she confides: "Since Leonardo's birth, I don't recognize myself. I, who am usually orderly in my business, responsible and structured; I forget obligations, I confuse dates, misplace things, etc. I seem to have given birth to my brain. [...] I feel like I am constantly in survival mode: my brain only retains the essential and rejects the superfluous. I have to remember so much information about the children that the rest fades away .... The storage limit has been reached!"

Now let's take a look at Instagram. On her account @lamatrescence (and the podcast of the same name), the sports journalist Clémentine Sarlat, then on air every day for Roland-Garros[6], writes:

"My body and especially my brain have limits. It has been two years since I've hosted a daily show. And wow, my head hurts. The number of times I confuse words/names of players.... Fortunately, now I know it's NORMAL and I'm doing the best I can. That's the main thing."

On social media the hashtag #mombrain is gathering thousands of posts, with many memes and jokes:

"My Saturday was going pretty well until I realized it was Sunday" @humanityinspires

"Also, on the list of things I can't remember: my own phone number. Instead I know the house phone number we had in 1992. Cool. Thanks. Awesome job brain." @mommacusses

"I don't mean to brag, but I can forget what I'm doing while I'm doing it." @mykidsbutler and others. I'm not really sure of the original source on this one.

"I'm at the point in parenting where 'What did I just say?!' could either be a threat or a genuine question" @katewouldhaveit

"My mind is like an internet browser. 19 tabs are open (at least 3 of them are frozen), and I have no idea where the music is coming from." @quinnandlaine

There are many, many posts like these that are related to what we call #mombrain or #mommybrain—the idea that we are losing our minds when we become mothers. One of my favorites that I use when I talk about the subject—which usually gets quite a few laughs out of the audience—is this: "I used to have functioning brain cells but I traded them in for children"—(origin unknown). But the question is: Is this true? Have we traded our brains in for children? Sometimes it may feel that way.

Before we get into the science of mothers' brains (because, yes, it is a real science) let's do a deep dive into what mommy brain is and how it is defined. If you google "mommy brain definition" you'll come up with the following:

- "The phenomenon known to mothers where their brains become useless piles of goo after being around their children for too long." (From the *Urban Dictionary* which I'm not sure is a real source for the English language). Really? That's a bit dramatic. It's obvious that our brains continue to function when we become parents. Otherwise we—and probably our children—would not survive.

- "A state in which a new mother is forgetful, absentminded, or easily distracted." This definition is from *YourDictionary* and seems to be a better definition of what we mean by mommy brain.

I should also point out that "mommy brain" is interchangeable with "pregnancy brain", "baby brain", "momnesia", or "mom brain". If you look up "baby brain" in the Cambridge Dictionary you'll find this definition "the condition of forgetting things and not being able to think clearly that pregnant women are often said to experience." So once a woman is expecting a baby she has no brain of her own, is that it? Don't worry, this isn't true!

In this book, I'll even convince you that when you become a mother, your brain gains superpowers. But for now, I want you to know that motherhood does change your brain and mostly in a good way.

But how would we summarize the term mommy brain? One could say that it is the feeling, experienced by many mothers, that their baby is literally sucking the cells out of their brains. This prevents them from thinking clearly, finding their words, remembering what they are talking about, remembering what they are doing, and more. Does that sound about right?

In the summer of 2019, American actress Anne Hathaway, who was nearing the end of her pregnancy, gave a great illustration of this as she answered a question during an interview. "My brain won't let me go there right now. I'm sorry," she explained with a laugh "Somebody's eating it.... I can focus on certain things that are fine, but there are certain things my brain refuses to allow me to imagine... directions....if you describe something, shapes, or you spell something, I can't go there. And certain words I have a tough time recalling, so I become that spinning wheel of death on your computer in conversations with me. I feel I'm very taxing for people to be around....If I haven't mentioned it, excuse me. I'm pregnant and I don't remember what I say from minute to minute."[7]

Clearly the experiences of mommy brain are real and likely don't spare many of us. Or, if you think you've escaped, maybe you forgot you had it. I remember during graduate school, when I started studying the relationship between memory and motherhood, I asked a friend who had recently had a baby if she had 'mommy brain'. She said, "oh no I didn't have any forgetfulness or problems with memory". Her husband turned and looked at her and said, "you would forget to put on your shoes if I didn't remind you" and that was followed by stories about how he did have to help her put on her shoes near the end of pregnancy as she had difficulty bending over.

Of course, not all women experience mommy brain in the same way and at the same level during pregnancy and the postpartum period. For me, it was the verbal memory—not being able to find the words for things. The words would be at the tip of my tongue and then *poof*: gone. And to be fair, nine years later I'm still forgetting my words, but perhaps that is a function of how many things I have going on in my day and less about hormones and parenting.

## A short history of mommy brain

We have a lot of anecdotes about our mom brain experiences that I could fill pages, but what I really want to talk about in this book is what the science says. This is where I began my research career. I was trying to figure out the science of mommy brain and what exactly happens to our memory when we become mothers. Are we really losing our memory and brain cells?

I started graduate school in 2002, before I had kids, at the University of Toronto. A few years earlier, I had completed a Bachelor of Science in Biopsychology at the University of British Columbia, and then took a couple of years off to work in a lab and manage a coffee shop. When I began my Masters degree in Toronto, I didn't know much about what so many women talked about as mommy brain, but I had always been intrigued with parenting, how the brain works and what physiological factors are important for mothering. When the opportunity arose to start a Master's degree and then PhD on motherhood, memory and hormones with Prof. Liisa Galea, I took it with the eagerness of any new graduate student. I delved into the literature and research. In 2002, there definitely wasn't as much in the news or on social media about mommy brain as there is today, but there was a bit of scientific research on this topic. It's one thing to talk about it, it's another thing to prove it.

The first account in the literature I can find on memory changes with motherhood was reported by Jean-Etienne Esquirol in *Mental Maladies; A treatise on Insanity* published 1838 in French. Born in 1772, Jean-Etienne Esquirol was a psychiatrist from Toulouse, France. In 1799, he began working at the Salpetriere Hospital in Paris where he developed a passion for mental illness. I'm definitely not talking about mommy brain as a mental illness here, but what is interesting is that in his book he talks about psychological struggles that women face when they become mothers. Of the 92 women he followed in his clinic, he reported that eight of them suffered from what he called postpartum dementia. In this context, we can think of dementia as a general term referring to loss of memory, language, problem-solving and other "thinking abilities" that are serious enough to interfere with daily life. In general, what we call mommy brain probably has some similarities with dementia, but don't worry, it's not dementia in the psychiatric sense. The point of sharing Jean-Etienne Esquirol's work is because it is the first record that I can find mentioning a problem of memory after childbirth. This was 1838 and I think he was onto something. However, it took over another 100 years before there was any research on how motherhood could affect memory and brain function.

From what I can find in the scientific literature, it was not until 1969 that the first research on memory and motherhood was published in a scientific journal. This research was part of a larger study on emotions and memory changes during pregnancy and the postpartum period, and

I will focus on the memory component here. In this study[8], 86 pregnant patients of the North Carolina Memorial Hospital, were asked about changes in their memory during pregnancy and the early postpartum period. This was done with questionnaires and interviews. The women interviewed were asked whether they felt foggy, if they felt unclear in their thinking, if they noticed any change in their ability to think, if there was change in their ability to concentrate, and if there was any difference in their memory function. Women were interviewed during pregnancy and again during the early postpartum period. Results of the study showed that 12-16% of women reported fogginess during pregnancy and postpartum. Interestingly, second-time mothers more often felt "fogginess" postpartum (31%) compared to first-time mothers (5%). This is perhaps not surprising as having two children at home definitely puts more demands on life.

This study is important and interesting because finally someone was looking at this topic. However, the measure of fogginess is fairly subjective and only one part of the experience of mommy brain, so of course, more research was needed. Another thing to point out in this study is that definitely 1 in 10 women reported fogginess during pregnancy or early motherhood, but was this level of fogginess different from what they felt before they were pregnant?

In reality, this study raises more questions than answers, but as I said, at that time the research was just getting started.

What happened next? It was nearly 20 years before another significant publication on the topic of mommy brain came out. Science can be so slow when it comes to motherhood research... In 1986, the first study specifically focused on mommy brain was published. The story goes that this study took place because a young neuropsychologist participating in a conference while six months pregnant noticed that she had serious changes in "intellectual functioning" and questioned whether other women experienced the same thing during pregnancy. In this study[9], 67 professional women (physicians, psychologists, nurses and administrators) were asked to fill out questionnaires indicating whether they noticed forgetfulness, disorientation, reading difficulties and confusion. The survey showed that 41% of the women participating in the study had one or more cognitive symptoms during pregnancy: the majority of these women reported having forgetfulness (80%) and reading difficulties (57%).

According to the authors these difficulties were not due to sleepiness, lack of concentration, irritability or lack of interest in their job. In fact, the authors of this study were so surprised by their findings that they gave this forgetfulness during pregnancy a medical term "benign encephalopathy of pregnancy" (a term which, thankfully, hasn't become popular today). They also recommended that professional women stop working if they suffered with this syndrome! But don't worry, research using objective tests of memory have shown a different story (I'll come back to this). And again, I should point out this study didn't compare the levels of forgetfulness or reading difficulties with how the women felt before they became mothers. It is therefore impossible to measure the importance of these results! One thing I appreciate about this study is the researchers' surprise that something so common as forgetfulness during pregnancy had never been reported in the scientific literature. They write that their "search of the world literature (all languages) did not turn up a single citation for the keywords forgetfulness, confusion, reading difficulty, disorientation, and cognitive difficulty occurring during pregnancy". (I, for one, am not surprised that there wasn't research on brain changes with motherhood before this. We often neglect investigating topics related to motherhood if they aren't directly related to the baby's well-being, and particularly when it comes to brain health.)

A few years after this research, another study, carried out in 1991[10], and based on a larger group (236 new mothers), showed that 82% of women experience what we call mommy brain during pregnancy and the postpartum period. In this study, reported changes included difficulty in concentration, absentmindedness and short-term memory loss. The authors investigated, more precisely, whether memory changes occur during pregnancy and the early postpartum period, and what type of memory changes were evident. They found that 50-64% of the women surveyed had experienced decreases in cognitive function, such as difficulty in concentrating on daily activities (reading, chores, conversation), difficulty remembering things, and feeling absent-minded. Interestingly, increased cognitive problems were associated with being older, married, living with a husband/partner, and having a higher level of education. Maybe this has to do with cognitive load or having one's brain constantly occupied. A further 50 pregnant women took part in another portion of this study and 82% of them reported general changes in memory, concentration, attention and increased absentmindedness.

Some women said "I lose concentration at work, forget simple instructions and muddle my words…I lose my keys and forget conversations…. I get into the car and forget where I'm driving to….".

These different studies clearly show that what is commonly called mommy brain (or what I prefer to call "memory changes with motherhood", because I think the real mommy brain is amazing) is a reality: moms definitely feel like they are forgetting things, have a lack of concentration, poorer attention and that they are in a kind of brain fog. One thing is certain, a majority of pregnant women and mothers in the early postpartum period feel a change in memory function; a change that is not welcome.

Are we losing our minds when we become mothers? No, but in reality the jury is still out on what mommy brain is. We do know that moms are feeling that their brains aren't functioning as they used to. The fact that your brain is changing is a good thing, because it has to change to learn how to take care of your baby. I like to think of mommy brain as all the things that change in your brain so that you can become a mom. I would argue that it is something positive; a new kind of superpower! But more on that later.

# Chapter 2.

# Is mommy brain a new thing?

At this stage of the book, we haven't yet defined the precise nature of mommy brain, but we know that many moms notice that some aspect of their memory is poorer during late pregnancy and the postpartum period. Before we delve into what types of memory actually change with motherhood, I'm curious to know if mommy brain is a new thing or not. Are we noticing memory changes that our mothers and grandmothers also noticed? Or is mommy brain dependent on our fast-paced society and pressures put on women to be a perfect mother?

## My Facebook research

To answer this question, I asked my family and friends on Facebook what they experienced (yes, Facebook. It's not the most popular platform, but I have a private account there where I keep in touch with my aunts, uncles, cousins, friends of the family, etc.)

I'm the youngest of four children, my father is the youngest of four, and I'm actually the youngest grandchild from my Pawluski side, so you can imagine that most of my cousins are well into their 50s and 60s and my aunts are in their 80s. This is a prime cohort to poll for some mommy brain information across the ages.

Here's what the over 70-year-olds said:

- "No. Don't remember anything like that."—Dianne P. (my aunt)

- "No also. I don't remember anything like that during pregnancy or any discussion of it. Sure remember it postpartum though!"—Nelda E. (second cousin)

- "No for me. I was one of the women who glowed through my pregnancies."—Judy P. (my aunt)

- "Except for morning sickness that lasted for months, I was good."—Sonya T. (another aunt)

I got a few more "No's", including from my mom. Of all the people who responded, only one remembered having memory troubles postpartum. From this, it looks like mommy brain may be a newer thing. Or maybe these women, many now in their late 70's or older, don't remember what it was like when they first had children!

The family and friends who became moms starting in the 1980s had more to say on the subject:

- "When I was pregnant, I had a lot of memory issues."—Barb C. (my cousin)

- "I have mentioned this several times with each pregnancy."—Jodi B.

- "Yes! I left my keys in the freezer! Forgot where I was going..."—Pauline M.

- "I always said pregnancy kills brain cells. It's been many moons so my memory isn't like it was. But I do remember being forgetful."—Laurie C. (my cousin)

By reading these different testimonies, we can easily see that mommy brain is most common for those that gave birth from the 1980s onwards. Why is that? Perhaps they have better memory for the past, which is, for them, more recent. Perhaps they were the ones who were more often working outside the home. Perhaps it's related to our progress in technology as a society. Perhaps it's all of these reasons. We don't know. And to be clear, this is a Facebook poll of my family and friends and not scientific research!

## Mommy brain and the mental load

It is difficult to know how long mothers have been suffering with perceptions of memory loss but here is something to think about: Since the industrial revolution, women have been contributing to the workforce outside of the home. It wasn't until the 1980s (yes, the 1980s) that a majority of the public—I'm talking about the USA here—approved of working wives (based on data from *Our World In Data*[11]). I imagine, with this approval of working wives, more women worked outside of the home... while of course managing to fulfill their roles as mothers! This role of mother is traditionally, and unfortunately still now, burdened with expectations of being the primary caregiver of children. This adds to the mental load or the number of things a mother has to do and think about every day. This can become exhausting very quickly! A mother who works outside of the home often doesn't come home from work to relax and watch some television. Coming home from work means starting her second shift: preparing dinner, finding Johnnie's football shoes, helping Isabelle with homework.... and the list goes on.

In *The Conflict: How Modern Motherhood Undermines the Status of Women*, Élisabeth Badinter[12] writes: "Our foremothers of the Enlightenment have bequeathed to us this unusual model of an emancipated woman of mothering, whose identity is not limited to motherhood." This is a good thing and it may be different from what happens in many other countries, but the fact remains that mothers still do most of the parenting and housework, even when they work outside the home. They must assume a mental load that can impact their memory and brain function.

This constant busy-ness can be a never-ending brain drain. We will talk more about mental load and memory in the coming chapters. Of course, this is speculation here, but I would predict that our mental load as mothers is heavier these days than it was in the past. Society has a lot of expectations on mothers and on how they raise their children. As mothers, we are expected to give our children every opportunity, which usually means coordinating a million activities per week, trying to juggle appointments, meetings, groceries and laundry between music, soccer and art classes. Often, these tasks are not fully shared with fathers/partners—who regularly have the better paying jobs, longer hours at work, and fewer expectations on their role as a parent.

I could probably discuss at length how much society—a patriarchal society—plays a role in how we feel as mothers today. But let's look at how motherhood and intelligence has been regarded. There has been a long tradition of women being seen as simple, not worthy of education, not able to be as intelligent as men. Mary Ann Evans, known by her pen name George Eliot, a leading writer of the Victorian era, wrote the following in *Adam Bede* (1859), "That's the way with these women— they've got no head-pieces to nourish, and so their food all runs either to fat or to brats". It's interesting how we still have memes today about our brains going to our children.

Of course, George Eliot's sentiment was written in a novel and may have been added for flair, but what about this quote from an Obstetrics textbook: "She (woman) has a head almost too small for intellect but just big enough for love."[13] Wow! This is pretty shocking to read when we know how remarkably intelligent women are. Perhaps Simone de Beauvoir sarcastically summed up the view of women best: "Woman? Very simply, say the fanciers of simple formulas: she is a womb, an ovary; she is a female—this word is sufficient to define her"[14].

According to Dr. Sarah Blaffer Hrdy, a leading anthropologist and author of *Mother Nature* (2000), for evolutionary theorists of the 1850s, women were there to reproduce, men were there to produce and thus, intelligence was not the role of the female. This bothers me for two reasons. First, the idea that men and women are different in the levels of intelligence is a ghastly idea which, thankfully, we know is untrue. Second, if women are only meant to reproduce this would imply that mothering doesn't require intelligence. Ridiculous. Mothering requires learning, creativity, time management, and a host of cognitive processes that are regularly overlooked but definitely evident. Obviously, this idea that mothers are not intelligent was put forth by men who didn't take an active role in parenting!

This is exactly what the French philosopher and scientist Clemence Royer, the first woman in France to be elected to a scientific society, LaSociete d'anthropologie de Paris, said in 1870: "Until now, science, like law, has been exclusively made by men and has considered woman too often an absolutely passive being...."[15] Today, things have changed with regards to the role of women in science, law and society, with more women taking active roles. However, we haven't come out from the shadow of the past yet.

In a study published in 2004, Dr. Amy Cuddy[16], a social psychologist, showed that when working women become mothers, they trade perceived competence for perceived warmth. In contrast, when working men become fathers they gain perceived warmth but maintain perceived competence. Simply put, this implies that when working women become mothers they are perceived as less intelligent. Oddly the same is not true for working men who become fathers. The study also shows that employers report less interest in hiring, promoting, and educating working mothers compared to working fathers or childless people.

Other research published in 2007[17] showed that pregnant women are often treated with hostility (e.g. with rudeness) when they are applying for a job. They are also "especially likely to encounter hostility when applying for masculine as compared to feminine jobs." This general hostility toward pregnant women seeking nontraditional roles may discourage pregnant women from pursuing work outside of perceived gender norms or societal expectations. I hate it when research confirms what we already know is true! How does this relate to mommy brain, you might ask?

Sometimes I wonder if we emphasize the memory issues with mommy brain because of history and our society's views that women are less intelligent, especially pregnant ones. Maybe when we start to notice memory changes as we become mothers, we become hyper-aware that they are there and forget to focus on all the amazing things we are accomplishing.

## Rebranding motherhood

One thing we can't deny is the idea that mothers are not smart, or smart enough, has trickled down into our societies and our unconscious. Perhaps this idea is the basis for Mommy Brain. To discover the truth, we need to know the facts, the objective facts, on how our intelligence changes with motherhood. What do the tests of memory say? Perhaps once we know this we can change how society thinks of mothers so it includes the incredible accomplishments that our brain (and body) achieve when we become mothers.

I would also argue that we need to rebrand motherhood: what it truly is and what it does. I have a quote from an Anne Klein advertisement on the wall in my office that I ripped out of a magazine left in the pocket of my seat on a transatlantic flight (where I had no movie access, the horror) and it reads, "Every human being is born out of the body of a woman". That is power. We need to remember that. Anna Malaika Tubbs, author of *The Three Mothers: How the Mothers of Martin Luther King, Jr., Malcolm X, and James Baldwin Shaped a Nation*[18], recently said it best in her essay in Mother Mag *We need to change the way we view motherhood*[19], "Mothers are holding and shaping the constant reimagining and evolution of our world, they deserve to be treated with the dignity and admiration that matches this capability." Mamas, you are doing amazing things.

Chapter 3.

# Mommy brain
# broken down

In the last few decades we've come a long way and, today, it is generally commonplace to talk about mommy brain and accept that it occurs. But what is it exactly? As I mentioned in Chapter 1, generally what we are talking about in terms of mommy brain is often a fogginess in our brains, with forgetfulness seeming to be the most popular complaint. Two questions come to mind for me from this description of mommy brain. 1) What is this forgetfulness that we experience? And 2) How does it differ from forgetfulness prior to motherhood?

## Zooming in on memory

Let's first talk about forgetfulness. You'll agree with me when I say that you can forget most anything, isn't that right? You can forget what you were going to say, you can forget a word to describe something, you can forget where you parked your car, you can forget your purse, and so on. Simply defined, forgetfulness is a failure to remember.

The loss of memory is much more complicated than we think. Prof. Elizabeth Loftus at the University of California, Irvine, has identified four major components of forgetting. It may be a failure to retrieve (information seems to have disappeared from your brain, and you can't get it back), memory interference (things get mixed up in your head), a lack of storage (you don't have enough space to keep information in memory) or a motivated forgetting (your brain decides to forget painful or traumatic information). And, of course, these components associated with forgetting rely on forming memories.

Memory itself is complex and can be broken down into key components. According to Inserm[20] it is defined as follows: "Memory makes it possible to record information from various experiences and events, to store and restore it. Different neural networks are involved in multiple forms of memory. Better knowledge of these processes improves understanding of certain memory disorders and opens the way to interventions with patients and their families. Memory is the function that allows us to integrate, retain and retrieve information to interact with our environment. It brings together skills, knowledge, memories. It is essential for reflection and projection into the future. It provides the basis of our identity."

It is also important to know that we have several types of memory. For example, remembering *where* we parked our car or put our grocery list would be spatial memory (memory of a spatial location). Remembering *what* we wanted to say or finding a word to say something would be a verbal memory. And then there is long-term and short-term memory and, of course, explicit and implicit memory. We can think of explicit memory as requiring effort (for example, your mother-in-law's birthday), whereas an implicit memory comes more easily (for example, the lyrics of your favorite song). In order to make memories, we also have to attend to things and have the space in our brains to store the memory. Therefore, attention as well as what we call cognitive load (the number of things that are going on) can also affect memory.

When moms say they are more forgetful or describe their brain as "foggy", what exactly is going on, and how different is their memory ability than women who are not moms? This is the question a few studies have asked since the early 1990s. I say "a few" because in reality this area of research is neglected. I am sure that if the majority of new fathers were talking about memory issues with fatherhood we would know much more about this subject!

## Memory during pregnancy: Is it really that bad?

Let's look at some of the research...The first objective study on memory and motherhood (by *objective,* I mean a study that actually gave moms and non-moms memory tests in a laboratory setting), was done in 1991[21]. Dr. Peter Brindle and his colleagues wanted to investigate whether women's feelings of being forgetful during pregnancy actually existed. The studies I talked about in Chapter 1 were subjective because they simply asked mothers if they felt like they had a change in their memory. These new studies measured certain memory abilities with standard tests of memory—objective tests. When doing this research in the lab, we have all the participants in the study (for example, pregnant and non-pregnant women) perform objective memory tests where the participant does a standardized task or fills out a questionnaire to assess aspects of their memory ability. Then the results of the groups are compared and statistically analyzed.

In the study of Brindle, the first objective study of memory in pregnancy, the researchers compared pregnant and non-pregnant women on two points: their perception of their memory ability (subjective study portion), as well as how they actually performed on memory tests (objective study portion). This was a great way to see if women's perception of their memory actually equated to their memory performance. Brindle and their team interviewed 41 women: 32 pregnant women and 9 non-pregnant women. This number of participants for a research study is small, but you have to start somewhere, as always. The researchers measured memory recall in the participants, that is, the ability to remember things seen a few minutes prior. At the start of the test, each participant was told that their memory for the items would be tested after a few minutes. The researchers showed the women 10 small household items and a list of words consisting of 12 names of kitchen utensils or fruit. Each item was presented successively at a rate of 1 per 2 seconds. After 2-4 minutes, they were asked to write down as many items as they could remember, in any order. This was a test of explicit memory—since it is active remembering or the conscious recall of facts.

Another test, a test for implicit memory, was also carried out. In other words, it is an unconscious memory or memory of how to do something without thinking, like shifting gears when driving a car. For this memory test, the researchers showed the participants a list of words that they didn't have to remember. Later, they were presented with the first

3 letters of the words and were asked to complete the word using the first word that came to mind. For example, they may have been presented with the word "bird" and a few minutes later were shown "bir".

The researchers found that "pregnant subjects were unimpaired compared to controls in tests of recall of household objects and of a list of words....". However, they found that pregnant women had a deficit in implicit memory that correlated with how they felt about their memory (subjective measures of memory). These findings suggest that when pregnant women report having poorer memory it's not because they can't learn things well, it's because they may have poorer memory for things that they didn't pay attention to. This study was an interesting start to memory and motherhood research, even if done on a small cohort of women. It shows that pregnant women are just as capable to learn and remember new things as non-pregnant women, if they have to do it.

## Memory postpartum: does it recover?

Let us now turn our attention to some of the first studies on mommy brain during the postpartum period. The first objective study on post-partum memory was in 1993[22]. Dr. Arthur Eidelman and his colleagues compared memory in 100 postpartum women (within 3 days of giving birth), 20 non-pregnant childless women, 15 late pregnant women at high-risk and in hospital, as well as 39 new fathers. They used different memory tests than in the study mentioned above, carried out by Brindle and colleagues.

The first test they used was a test of verbal memory. A researcher read two unrelated paragraphs to the participant and then asked them to remember as many of the details as possible. A second test of memory focused on aspects of visuospatial memory (Wechsler tests). The participants viewed three abstract figures for 10 seconds each and then they were asked to draw the figures from memory after each presentation.

In this study, the researchers found that on the first day postpartum, mothers did worse on the memory tests (verbal and visuospatial) compared to nonpregnant women, but on postpartum days 2 and 3, their performance was the same as nonpregnant women. Interestingly, fathers scored significantly lower than nonpregnant women on the verbal memory test the day after the birth of their child. Pregnant women also did worse on the verbal memory test than non-pregnant women. On the second test, the visuo-spatial memory test, no differences were shown between the groups.

In summary, these early studies are evidence that memory changes reported by mothers during pregnancy and the early postpartum period exist, but not on all aspects of memory. In the subsequent decades, additional research, although sparse, has been carried out with a mix of results, potentially confusing things further. As one researcher said, "the overall picture is one of consistency in *reported* memory changes or cognitive changes, but *uncertainty* about the nature of any objective change in cognitive performance."[23]

## Are the changes in memory as big as they seem?

A number of reasons could explain the discrepancies in our understanding of exactly what happens in terms of memory during pregnancy and the postpartum period. Probably some of the primary issues with this research is that there isn't much research on this subject and the research that has been done uses different tests of memory in different ways, or at different time points in pregnancy or postpartum, or the number of participants in the studies is low... In short, the list of explications is long!

To make sense of the mixed results in the sparse literature on mommy brain, the Australian researchers Dr. Julie Henry and Dr. Peter Rendell decided to do a type of summary of the research (called a meta-analysis). They published their work in 2007[24]. At that time, there were only 17 published studies where objective memory tests were used to look at memory in mothers and compare it to memory in non-mothers. Seventeen studies in 20 years, that's very little. Especially, if you put it in perspective with the fact that up to 80% of women complain of forgetfulness or fogginess during pregnancy and the early postpartum period. On average 80% of women will get pregnant in their lifetime. That's a huge portion of the population who will struggle with mommy brain, yet we still don't know much about it! Again, I ask myself the question: would things be different if new fathers complained of memory problems? Definitely.

But back to the meta-analysis of Henry and Rendell. They compiled the results of the 17 studies to see if there are memory differences between pregnant and nonpregnant women. This is a great way to see what effects in the scientific literature may actually apply to the general population. Their conclusions, after the analysis of the 17 studies measuring different types of memory in women during pregnancy and the postpartum period, indicate that pregnancy and the postpartum period show deficits in specific types of memory such as free recall (the ability to remember a list of words or items after viewing them recently) and some aspects of working memory (the ability to temporarily retain information). They also found that memory types that require attention and effort to learn can be negatively affected. But don't panic, don't believe you have completely lost your memory! The authors note that the magnitude of these memory deficits is small and subtle. They suggest that these changes likely have minimal effects on carrying out tasks at work or at home.

Since 2007, further research on memory and motherhood, although limited, has looked at different types of memory, and, again, with mixed results. For example, in a longitudinal study Dr. Helen Christensen and colleagues looked at whether pregnancy and motherhood were associated with brief or long-term cognitive changes by testing memory before pregnancy and during motherhood. These results expand those of Henry and Rendell, and the authors conclude that: "Not so long ago pregnancy was 'confinement' and motherhood meant the end of career aspirations. Our results challenge the view that mothers are anything other than the intellectual peers of their contemporaries."[25] I agree! In the following chapters, I will talk a bit more about the areas of memory and motherhood that need more research. But from the research I've talked about so far, I'm confident that our brains don't go to mush when we become mothers.

## Remembering to do things

When I was in graduate school, I was a co-author on a study led by Dr. Carrie Cuttler, where we investigated prospective memory during pregnancy. Prospective memory involves remembering to do something at some point in the future. For example, remembering to call your mom on her birthday. In this study, we asked 61 pregnant and 24 non-pregnant women to do objective and subjective memory tests in the laboratory as well as prospective memory tests from home, such as calling the lab to confirm their study appointment. What we found in the study is that when asked to do objective memory tests in the lab, pregnant women performed just as well as non-pregnant women, even though pregnant women reported that they felt that their memory was worse. Interestingly, we found when doing the memory test at home pregnant women had deficits in memory compared to non-pregnant women. What we concluded from this study was that "pregnant women experience everyday life problems with memory that are not readily detected in the laboratory environments."[26] I believe this is a key aspect of mommy brain that we need to explore—how memory works in our home environments.

# Chapter 4.

# Why do we have mommy brain?

N ow that we know about the first scientific studies on the subject, we can ask ourselves why we have memory changes when we become mothers. There are likely many reasons for this, but let's talk about the most popular and significant ones here, and note that they are possibly all interrelated. As always, when talking about the brain, things can get complex. So, I'm going to simplify things and break them down here into five areas: the brain, hormones, sleep, mood and nutrition.

## The brain

It's impossible to talk about mommy brain without talking about how it may be linked to changes in a mother's brain. A funny thing is that we don't have much research on how mommy brain (memory and motherhood) is related to brain changes. Motherhood is linked to a host of fascinating brain changes that are important for mothering, which we'll talk about in Part 2. But if we're talking just about mommy brain, is the idea that a mother's brain has turned to mush or that a mother has traded in functioning brain cells for children, really true?

When I started out in this area of research in 2002, there was maybe one study looking at memory during pregnancy and how it related to brain changes. This study was done by my PhD supervisor, Prof. Liisa Galea, at the University of British Columbia, and it was carried out in pregnant rats. I didn't mention it before, but the majority of what we know about the maternal brain is from these laboratory rodents. They have amazing maternal behaviors and we can look in detail at what is going on in their brains—something we can't do in humans where usually only volume or activity of the brain is investigated. We also know that there are many similarities in the brains of all mammals which makes using non-human mammals for research valuable.

What Liisa found was that when tested on a spatial memory test, there was a decrease in memory in these female rats the further along in their pregnancy they progressed[27]. When she looked at the brain area most related to spatial memory functioning, the hippocampus (which is probably my favorite brain area), she found that the size of the hippocampus had decreased in these pregnant females that had poorer spatial memory. This was the first direct link between memory and brain functioning in pregnancy.

Now, I'm sure you're all thinking, "see the brain does decrease in size as it prepares for children." But not so fast! There is more going on than you think, especially when we talk about maternal care and bonding to your infant. Since this first study on pregnant rats carried out by Liisa and her colleagues, research that I have done in rat moms shows that a decrease in the production of new neurons in the hippocampus is associated with an increase in memory performance later in the postpartum[28]. With this, I'm guessing that you are lost. What is clear is there are differences during pregnancy and the postpartum period in how memory is affected and how the brain may be mediating those changes. If you want to learn more about this time course of mommy brain and how long it lasts, stay tuned, I'll cover that in the next chapter. For now, let's revisit how the brain may be involved in memory changes with motherhood.

In 2017 there was an interesting study[29] published on how pregnancy changes a woman's brain. I'm sure you read about it at some point, as it had international coverage for its remarkable findings. This research was headed by Dr. Elseline Hoekzema and Dr. Susana Carmona at the University of Madrid[30]. They found that from before pregnancy until a few weeks after birth, there is a decrease in the volume of a number of brain areas associated with social behaviors and mothering. I think when this research was published, a lot of women had a sigh of relief because they could say "see, my brain is shrinking", that's the problem. I spoke with

Elseline on my podcast *Mommy Brain Revisited*[31] about this research and its implications for mommy brain. What she reminded me of was the data: She found that even though many brain areas important for social behavior and even some for memory (i.e. the hippocampus) were smaller in size after giving birth, there were no differences in memory performance between moms and non-moms in the study. Furthermore, the decrease in brain area size was not associated with memory performance at all, at least not on the tests of memory they used. Even more interesting was that the researchers found the smaller the brain area volumes, the greater the feelings of attachment a mother felt toward her infant. Pretty amazing, right? Less is more, at least when it comes to your brain on kids.

It's also important to note that after birth, the size of the hippocampus (a brain area essential for memory) wasn't related to those aspects of memory that were investigated in this study—those being verbal memory and working memory. On a side note, I can tell you that Elseline, as with so many moms, experienced mommy brain herself, particularly with regards to verbal memory deficits. We joked about this the last time we talked, but one thing she pointed out was that, for her, being a mom is amazing and worth it—even when experiencing some problems with memory.

Another recent study[32] conducted at the University of Guadalajara, Mexico, used the electroencephalogram (EEG) to look at brain activity and memory in pregnant women. This technique makes it possible to measure electrical activity of the cortical areas of the brain using small, metal discs (electrodes) that are attached to various positions on the scalp. Brain cells communicate via electrical impulses all the time, so this measurement gives an indication of brain activity in response to stimuli, such as a picture. The study showed that pregnancy has a minimal effect on memory—and in this case they were looking at visuospatial working memory, which is the ability to remember an object and its location. However, with respect to brain functionality, pregnant women (and not non-pregnant women) had specific patterns of EEG activity between the prefrontal and parietal cortices of the brain while performing the memory tasks. The authors proposed that "pregnancy could represent adaptive mechanisms" that enable pregnant women to focus their attention on performing memory tasks. This seems to put pregnancy-related brain changes and memory performance in a positive light, but still we are in our infancy in terms of what exactly is going on in our brains when we experience memory changes with motherhood.

## Hormones

Ah, hormones....we love to blame a women's problems on hormones. Mommy brain is no exception, but let's see what the science says. I'm guessing we all know that hormones change during pregnancy and the postpartum period, but here's a brief refresher. The levels of steroid hormones, of which estradiol and progesterone are the most popular, increase up to 100 times during pregnancy (depending on the hormone you're talking about). The increase in these hormones is largely due to the placenta and, of course, the need to remain pregnant. During the end of pregnancy there is a normal increase in cortisol, another steroid hormone, which helps to prepare the mother and baby for labor and birth. By the way, there are many other hormones, neurotransmitters and physiological factors that change with pregnancy, but I'm going to focus on the most obvious ones and how they may relate to memory. Birth happens and a lot goes on there, to say the least. After birth, the levels of steroid hormones plummet and the peptide hormones, oxytocin and prolactin, rise, particularly if you are breastfeeding (but both hormones are also important for other things besides breastfeeding).

These same hormones, particularly the steroid hormones, have been implicated in memory function at other times in a woman's life. For example, estradiol has a protective effect on verbal and working memory in women who are cycling or postmenopausal. Therefore, it makes sense that estradiol may be a key player in mommy brain. However, the research hasn't been able to link maternal memory with changes in the concentration of this, or other hormones. Research by Dr. John Buckwalter and colleagues, in the late 90s[33], showed that although pregnant women report memory deficits, particularly in aspects of verbal memory, none of the hormone levels they looked at were associated with these changes in memory. These hormones included estradiol, progesterone, cortisol, testosterone and dehydroepiandrosterone (DHEA), a steroid hormone precursor.

Often the relationship between hormones and memory is not linear but, instead, is in an inverted-U shape where high or low levels of a hormone can be detrimental, whereas moderate hormone levels can be beneficial. To investigate this relationship further in the context of mommy brain, Prof. Barbara Sherwin's group at McGill University[34] showed that cortisol levels were associated with verbal memory during pregnancy and the early postpartum period in an inverted-U shaped fashion such that moderate levels of cortisol were beneficial for memory performance. They also found that prolactin levels during pregnancy were associated with tests of memory recall, suggesting that more than just the steroid hormones may be related to memory changes with motherhood. Apart from looking at memory tasks, this study looked at aspects associated with memory, such as attention, and found that lower levels of estradiol and cortisol postpartum were associated with better attention. However, other research on different aspects of memory, such as prospective memory, has not shown a link with cortisol levels in pregnancy.

Research in animal models more clearly points to a relationship between hormones and memory in parents, particularly with a focus on cortisol. A recent study[35] out of Prof. Kelly Lambert's lab at the University of Richmond showed that captive mother and father Owl Monkeys, which are small New World monkeys aptly named for their huge owl-like wide eyes, are better at performing a memory task which relies on foraging. They also found that the monkey parents have higher DHEA to cortisol ratio, which suggests a potential link between hormones and memory. Research that I did for my dissertation also points to a link between increases in cortisol and memory in mothers during the postpartum period[36], but much more research is needed in this area.

There is also research pointing to a role of brain oxytocin levels in memory performance postpartum. This work was carried out in the laboratory of Prof. Benedetta Leuner at The Ohio State University. In her study[37], which was done in rat mothers, she investigated cognitive flexibility. Cognitive flexibility is the ability to switch between thinking about two or more different things. It's something I think most mothers do on a regular basis. What she found was that mother rats were better at cognitive flexibility than virgin rats, which perhaps isn't a surprise, but she also found that the action of oxytocin in the prefrontal cortex is important for the ability of the mothers to multitask.

Taken together this suggests that both the steroid and peptide hormones are important for different aspects of memory during pregnancy and the postpartum period.

When talking about hormones, I think it's also important to talk about the idea that fetal sex can impact memory during motherhood. Wow, right? To my knowledge, only one study in humans has explored this possibility, but it is an interesting idea since we know that fetal sex can affect the hormones of pregnancy. This study[38] was published when I was in graduate school by a group at the other university in town— Simon Fraser University in Vancouver. The work was out of Prof. Neil Watson's lab. I've had the pleasure of meeting Neil on a number of occasions to talk about this and other research that he is involved in (Coincidently, I was given kids' books by a Vancouver illustrator as a gift for my daughter which feature Neil's daughter as one of the main characters. These books are called *Haley and Bix* and are great for kids). Back to science—what Neil and his student at the time, Claire Vanson, showed was that across pregnancy (in women with no knowledge of the sex of their fetus) and the early postpartum period, women who gave birth to boys did significantly better than women who gave birth to girls on three of the most difficult objective memory tests they were asked to perform in the lab. Also note, that overall memory performance on these tasks did not differ with those of non-pregnant women.

It seems plausible to think that hormones derived from the male or female fetus may be contributing to these memory changes. However, the authors point out that there is limited evidence that fetal hormones (primarily testosterone in male fetuses) may be altering maternal memory. For example, the present study found that at about 10 weeks of fetal age, a difference in maternal memory started to occur, before the mothers knew the sex of the fetus, and before the peak in testosterone levels by male fetuses (which peaks between 15-18 weeks of gestation). One thing the authors do suggest is that this fetal sex effect on maternal memory may be due to human chorionic gonadotropin (hCG) levels. hCG is significantly elevated in women pregnant with female fetuses and this difference is evident early in pregnancy—as early as 3 weeks after fertilization. hCG is a hormone important for the maintenance of pregnancy and it readily gets into the brain and can interact with brain areas important for memory performance.

Whether or not we notice the impact of the sex of our babies on our memory is another question. I had one of each (a girl and a boy) and I'm not sure if that made a difference. This leads me to wonder what the situation is for twins or multiples when it comes to mommy brain; another wide open area to explore!

In summary, we don't have a very good understanding of the role of hormones on memory in mothers (and maybe because we don't know much about motherhood and memory, in general). Certain hormones appear to be important for some aspects of memory during pregnancy or postpartum, but it's not as clear as we would like it to be. One thing is for sure: it is impossible to say that memory changes with motherhood are only due to hormones. Let's continue our investigation...

## Sleep

It may seem obvious that sleep plays a role in mommy brain. Many studies on aspects of memory and motherhood take sleep into account by asking participants about their sleep, and using a sleep questionnaire to quantify sleep patterns and experiences. But despite what seems like the obvious, a consistent effect of sleep on memory during pregnancy or postpartum has not been reported, at least on the tests used in the laboratory.

There is an interesting study of note here though[39]. Dr. Annette Swain and her colleagues compared the performance of mothers in the early postpartum period and mothers not in the postpartum period, but who had children under five years of age, who slept through the night. Researchers gave all the women memory and concentration tests and they found that new postpartum mothers (within three weeks of giving birth) had poorer sleep compared to mothers that had older children who slept through the night (not a surprise here). Interestingly, even though sleep was disturbed in the mothers in the early postpartum period, no differences were found between these group of mothers (new and experienced) on measures of memory or attention tested in the study.

What is important to note about sleep and memory in this study is that a new mother's performance on memory tests was related to the amount of sleep she received the night before the test. This same relationship between sleep and memory was not evident in mothers whose older children slept through the night.

Thus, sleep can play an important role in some aspects of memory, at least in the early postpartum period. Despite this, I'm always surprised what new parents can achieve while sleep deprived. I know my husband has mentioned, on more than one occasion, that he can do much more now as a sleep-deprived parent, than he could as a sleep-deprived pre-parent. I guess, as parents, we quickly learn that the luxury of getting more sleep is often not possible and we adapt. Regardless, I think there is more of a link between sleep and mommy brain than the science has shown us so far. More research please!

## Mood

Recent research suggests that mood is linked to mommy brain but, again, the research is inconclusive. One recent study, that is interesting to note here, is from Dr. Helena Rutherford's group at Yale[40,41]. In this study, the researchers looked at the interplay between memory, mood and response to an infant in distress. Sixty-one mothers participated in this study. They were asked to come to the lab where they were given tests of working memory and emotional regulation. Their behavioral responsivity to an infant in distress was also observed. Rest assured that no infant was traumatized during this study, the researchers used a simulator which had the appearance of an infant. The premise of this research was that improved working memory performance is important for managing our emotions, as shown in other research, and that these factors may be associated with how a mother responds to her infant. The researchers found something interesting—better working memory performance in the mothers, through its role in increasing maternal emotional regulation, predicted a delay in responding to the crying baby simulator. Hold on a second, that seems counterintuitive? To me, it suggests that mothers that have better emotional regulation (for example, positive self-talk), which is associated with better working memory, are not as emotionally reactive (or stressed) in responding to an infant in distress. Clearly, there is an interaction between memory, emotions and parenting that further research needs to explore in detail.

It's not surprising to think that mommy brain and mood are linked, but often, when women talk about it they are frustrated or amused with how they are feeling and are not suffering from a mental illness. However, if chronic and persistent memory deficits exist along with a persistent change in mood (sadness, anxiety, anger) then it is necessary to speak with a health care provider. I will return to the theme of mood and motherhood in Part 4.

## Nutrition

Is there a link between mommy brain and nutrition? I am sure there is, to a degree. But at this point we need more research to support this idea. In the 1980s, there were two small studies on this subject, and I have yet to see much more on the literature today. One of these studies[42], showed that pregnant women receiving iron supplements had better short-term memory and attention. The other study[43], showed that a reduction in caffeine intake was associated with poorer memory performance during pregnancy (it's important to note that this study only involved 6 women, so replication is definitely needed).

Today, we know that nutrition, in general, plays a role in memory. I'm sure we've all seen those ads for fish oil or omega 3s, and their role in improving memory. There is plenty of science backing up how certain nutrients found in our diet can improve memory processes and attention. This is not new. More recently, research has focused on the link between gut microbiota and memory[44]—an exciting area of research. But what we don't know is exactly how nutrition or our gut microbiota affects memory during motherhood. Again, more research on this topic is needed.

In this chapter, I've briefly covered some key points that may explain the changes in memory that so many mothers talk about. Of course, these factors, and others that may play a role, need to be investigated in more detail. I would sum things up by saying that there is uncertainty about the mechanisms that underlie the memory deficits observed during pregnancy and the postpartum period, and uncertainty about the exact nature of these deficits. Various factors have been attributed to mommy brain and these include brain changes, complex hormonal changes that take place during pregnancy and birth[45], changes in mood[46] but also cultural stereotypes around motherhood[47]. Bottom line, expecting motherhood to cause memory deficits can make you forget all the amazing things your brain is doing when you become a mother.

# Chapter 5.

# Mommy brain always?

"Mom Brain—That forgetful and somewhat confusing part of motherhood that begins with your first pregnancy and ends when you die" @macgyveringmom 22.

Can we really define mommy brain like that? Have we lost our minds or our memory forever? Let's look at the evidence. The previous chapters showed that, yes, our feelings of having memory troubles during pregnancy and the early postpartum are valid, and they likely exist for various reasons. However, we still don't know a great deal about these memory changes. A bigger question that often arises is not what mommy brain is, but will it last forever?!

## When does it start during pregnancy?

First of all, let's see when mommy brain starts and look at it as a timeline. In the same way that pregnancy involves trimesters and the postpartum is ever changing (especially the first year), it seems like feelings of mommy brain follow this same trajectory. Of course, rarely has the research on memory and motherhood consistently studied women during all three trimesters and into the postpartum year, and beyond. However, a meta-analysis[48] published in 2018 by Sasha Davies[49] and colleagues at Deakin University in Australia investigated the research on this subject across the three trimesters of pregnancy. They determined when mommy brain starts, when it is the most intense, specific memory performance, and executive function (processing speed, verbal, visuospatial abilities) in pregnant and non-pregnant never mothered women. The researchers found that, overall, when looking at all these factors together, cognitive functioning was poorer in pregnant women than a non-pregnant woman. They also concluded that cognitive functioning, working memory and memory recall were poorer in women during late pregnancy, compared to non-pregnant women—and significantly for women in their third trimester of pregnancy. For example, they found impairment in executive functions, which include things like paying attention and planning, shifting between ideas (flexibility), and problem-solving in pregnant women compared to non-pregnant women (but I should mention here, again, that there are very few studies in this area). In summary, the data from this meta-analysis shows that memory and other cognitive functions, such as attention and shifting between ideas, is poorer in pregnant women than a non-pregnant woman, particularly during the third trimester. This decline in memory begins towards the end of the first trimester (at least in the few studies that are reported here).

It is important to note, that while there were differences in memory performance of pregnant and non-pregnant women, these differences were generally small. They could, for example, result in forgetting or failing to book a hair appointment, but they do not appear to be things that significantly interfere with job performance or the ability to perform complex tasks. In fact, the researchers report that "the impact of these effects on the quality of life and everyday functioning of pregnant women requires further investigation."

What also may be striking is that even studies in laboratory rats show deficits in memory during late pregnancy and the early postpartum period. For example, my PhD supervisor published a study in 2000[50] where she looked at the effects of pregnancy on memory in rats. She used a task where animals had to use the cues in the room (pictures on the walls for example) to remember where a hidden platform was in a pool of opaque water. Rats are natural swimmers, but they don't want to swim forever. In this memory task, called the Morris Water Maze, rats learn where a hidden platform is under the water so they can stand and take a break from swimming. After they learn where the platform is, a few hours or even the next day or two, they are put back into the same pool of water and the time it takes them to find the hidden platform is measured. This is a form of spatial memory (memory for a place). This study found that during late pregnancy (the last week of the normal

3 weeks gestation in a rat), pregnant females took longer to reach the hidden platform compared to non-pregnant females, despite swimming at the same speed as non-pregnant females. Even pregnant rats have poorer memory sometimes!

## How long do these changes last?

Now we know when mommy brain seems to start, in general—the end of the first trimester there can be some slight changes—and it is on average more marked in late pregnancy, then what happens after birth? The postpartum is also an ever-changing period, not divided into trimesters as pregnancy is, but it definitely changes as the baby grows. The subtle memory deficits in mothers at the beginning of the postpartum period, which I've already talked about, are also reported in rodent models. For example, in 2007 Prof. Muriel Darnaudery, now at the University of Bordeaux, showed deficits in spatial memory in the mother rat at the start of the postpartum period[51], similar to what was shown during late pregnancy in the rat, in the study mentioned above. Again, this decrease in memory with motherhood is showing a similar profile to what we are seeing in women (but which needs more research for clarification) and suggests an evolutionary conserved effect of motherhood on the mammalian brain.

I think that a more pressing question is how long into the postpartum do these changes in memory last? Before we delve into the literature, I want to address (quickly) the question of breastfeeding: can it have an impact on mommy brain? Some people say that mommy brain postpartum is breastfeeding brain for those that are breastfeeding. In *The Female Brain*, author Louann Brizendine, MD writes, "...one downside of breastfeeding can be a lack of mental focus. Although a fuzzy brained state is pretty common after giving birth, breastfeeding can heighten and prolong this mellow...unfocused state...the parts of the brain responsible for focus and concentration are preoccupied with protecting and tracking the newborn". As far as the research is concerned, I'm not sure there is clear consensus on whether breast versus bottle feeding differentially impact a mother's memory. I haven't seen any data on this subject. So, either it doesn't exist, or more research is needed.

Let's now look at mommy brain postpartum. In the 1990s, when research on this subject really got underway, there was a ground-breaking study in rats that suggested the complete opposite. It suggested that memory impairment with motherhood doesn't exist and, quite the contrary, that motherhood makes you smarter. Yes, you read that right! This study, headed by the late Prof. Craig Kinsley, was published in 1999 in *Nature*[52], a distinguished science journal. It showed that in experienced mother rats (rats that had had at least two litters) there was an enhancement in working memory performance compared to rats that had never mothered. Their work even showed that adopting offspring for a couple of weeks improved a female's working memory performance. In addition, weeks after weaning of offspring, this improvement in memory was still evident in mother rats.

Interestingly, Craig told Quartz.com[53] that his research was inspired by watching his wife shortly after giving birth. "I noticed my wife becoming much more efficient and able to do everything she did before, plus take care of a new baby. I put these ideas into the lab and started testing them and it was just like finding a gold mine." I'm not sure we all are as efficient as Craig's wife after our first-born, but his research started a conversation about the benefits of motherhood for mommy brain. Craig and I never had the chance to talk about this inspiration for his research, but I had the chance to meet him on several occasions and work with him on a review of motherhood and the hippocampus[54] (a brain area important for learning and memory). He was a champion for maternal brain research and a man truly fascinated by the impact of motherhood on the mother. His enthusiasm for this research is not forgotten and has inspired many of us in the field.

Craig's 1999 study became the foundation of my PhD work where I investigated the impact of mothering experience on memory and the hippocampus in mother rats. My research started to answer the question of whether this improvement in memory after weaning in first-time moms was better than in age-matched second-time mothers, compared to non-mother rats. I also investigated whether it was pregnancy alone, or the experience of mothering (via adoption), that was important for these memory effects with motherhood. For this, I used a different memory test than the Morris Water Maze mentioned above: the radial arm maze. This maze is a kind of 'sun' with a centre and eight arms projecting from the centre section. Four of the arms are baited with food, and the rat learns to use cues on the wall (colored shapes and pictures) to remember which arms of the maze have food and which do not. For a food reward, we used a piece of a breakfast cereal (Froot Loops). Rats love these fruit loop treats and are very motivated to remember where they are.

From this research, published in 2006[55], I found that first-time mother rats have better memory than rats that are not mothers. I also found that second-time mothers (of the same age) have improved memory compared to non-mother rats but they do not perform as well as first-time mothers. There is something special about the first time as a mother. My research also showed that this enhancement in spatial memory in first-time moms lasted at least 2 months after giving birth in the rat—which is quite a long time—and appears to be due to a combination of the effects of pregnancy and mothering, and not pregnancy or mothering alone. The combination of pregnancy and mothering is important. I also want to point out that these memory improvements in the postpartum rat mom were observed when the moms were no longer lactating and no longer had offspring to care for. This is likely a key point to think about.

## Memory improvements with age?

Human research has yet to parallel the animal research and confirm when during the postpartum period, or after weaning, mommy brain improves. Or better yet, explore what cognitive capacities are better with motherhood throughout pregnancy, the early postpartum years, and further on into motherhood (when children are in daycare or school). In 1999, a study[56] showed that at two months postpartum cognitive performance of new mothers is a bit better than during late pregnancy. The same researchers went on to show, in a very small study (with only 11 participants)[57], that at two years postpartum there is an improvement in cognitive abilities in mothers, compared to during late pregnancy and the early postpartum. This suggests a possible enhancing effect of motherhood on memory.

Dr. Valerie Miller, at Purdue University in Indiana, recently looked at maternal attention in the postpartum period, a few years after childbirth. Attention is an important component of memory and it would make sense that improved attention may be associated with improved memory. In her research, published in 2020[58], memory wasn't assessed, but what Valerie found was that later in the postpartum period (on average at 3.5 years), in women who were no longer breastfeeding, there was improved control of attention as measured by laboratory tests. To sum it up nicely Valerie told me on my podcast *Mommy Brain Revisited*[59] that "Moms are better at ignoring the things they need to ignore in order to focus". That sounds about right—as mothers, if we need to focus, we can.

Attention is enhanced in the years following birth, but what about memory? The first studies on the enduring effects of motherhood on memory were, not surprisingly, done in rat moms. Again, Prof. Craig Kinsley pioneered this work by showing that rats that had been mothers, performed better on memory tasks well into aging[60] (at 2 years of age with the average life of a Sprague-Dawley rat being 3 years). This finding has been replicated in a few other studies in rats, which showed that not only memory, but also the ability to switch from task to task, is enhanced in rats that have mothered[61].

But what about in women? Does this enhancement in memory with motherhood exist later in life? Very recent work suggests it does. A study led by Dr. Kaida Ning and their colleagues at the University of Southern California[62] looked at visual memory in mothers and fathers (note that visual memory in motherhood has not often been the focus of research, although it's been suggested that pregnancy changes visual acuity). In this study, the authors report that 50-year-old mothers and fathers, who had children years earlier, have better visual memory than nonparents. In fact, they report that parents who had two or three children performed much better on a visual memory task than childless adults. This research suggests that in both parents, the act of parenting, and not the physical process of pregnancy, contributes to these enhancements in visual memory. According to the authors, reasons for these improvements in memory with parenting may be explained as follows: "Having offspring is associated with significant life changes, which may improve brain health directly or indirectly. First, having offspring is associated with a healthier lifestyle, such as less frequent use of alcohol and tobacco, and more regular mealtimes. Second, children might serve as a bridge connecting parents to more social and community activities, which improves cognitive function. Third, adult children can provide parents with emotional and social support, as well as instrumental support such as shopping and housework." The authors also acknowledge that further research is needed to determine the link between parenting, the environment, and improved visual memory.

Even into our 70s, motherhood is associated with improvements in memory. In a recent study[63] Dr. Winnie Orchard and colleagues at Monash University in Australia, showed that mothers averaging 70 years of age performed better on a verbal memory task than non-mothers of the same age, and that this memory improved with the number of children a woman mothered. Crazy, right? But it's true. The researchers did not find the same effects in 70-year old fathers. This may be due to gender norms at the time and other cultural factors.

I have to admit that I'm a bit jealous of my friend who has seven kids. Apparently, her memory will be excellent when she gets older!

In summary, when does mommy brain (aka memory deficits with motherhood) peak and when does motherhood make us smarter? The science says mommy brain peaks during late pregnancy and the early postpartum period and maybe again with a second child. As a mother of two—thinking back on when my mommy brain peaked—I'd have to say that I noticed it significantly during the second trimester of my first pregnancy. Perhaps it subsided a bit postpartum, but it then picked up again when I had my second, with two kids under 2 years old. It's seven years after my second/last child and I have to say that I still feel like I have some verbal memory deficits, but I'm not sure if that's due to kids or to life, in general. Regardless, any mommy brain I've experienced has been well worth it and I wouldn't change it for the world.

Chapter 6.

# Rebranding mommy brain

A few years ago, I came across an article in *Today's Parent* originally titled *Baby Brain is BS and motherhood actually makes you smarter*[64] (in other words : *mommy brain is bullshit and motherhood makes us more intelligent*). Mommy brain is bullshit?! What the hell? Sure, we don't know much about mommy brain, but when 80% of women talk about some sort of memory decline during pregnancy or the post-partum there has to be something to it. I was shocked that someone would write something like this, especially given the science, although sparse. When you start telling people that something they experience does not exist you start to silence them and not give them a space to express their concerns. I shared this with the author of this article and sent her studies in humans and animals showing that, yes, there are real memory deficits with pregnancy and the early postpartum. These deficits are not huge, but they are there in the research. We exchanged several rather heated emails, but unfortunately, nothing changed in the article.

Do I think motherhood makes us smarter? Definitely! You have to learn how to keep a baby alive. That's a huge task that involves different types of memory and a host of cognitive and emotional changes. Not all memory is negatively affected by motherhood. In fact, very few types are, we just seem to focus on them. One of my favorite studies[65] shows, for example, that after just a few hours spent with their newborn, mothers and fathers can recognize their infant simply by touching the back of their infant's hand (when given a choice of three hands from three infants). Think how amazing that is. Wow! (Go ahead, try it next time you're with friends and their kids, and tell me how it turns out...). Unfortunately, we often focus on memory deficits and don't talk about those amazing things a mother's brain does. This is something I hope will change.

## Unconscious bias

I've already talked about the research. In summary, memory problems during late pregnancy and the postpartum do exist—particularly for certain types of memory, such as finding the words for things or remembering something you needed to do a few minutes or hours ago. Are they huge memory changes that interfere with our daily lives in a serious fashion? No. If pregnant women really struggled with memory deficits, I bet newspapers would be full of headlines like "Pregnant Women Gets Lost Again and Doesn't Know Where She Is" or "Pregnant Doctor Repeatedly Gives Wrong Prescription to Patients". Imagine the horror of that! Think about it—how many pregnant or early postpartum professional women remain competent and successful at their jobs? Without a doubt, most of them.

Why, then, do we talk so much about mommy brain, especially in the anglophone world, but also more and more often elsewhere? Women for centuries have been seen as the "weaker sex", the sex that is not as smart. This discrimination happens every day in one way or another. In 2017, Polish MP Janusz Korwin-Mikke declared before the Polish Parliament, during a debate on the wage gap between women and men, "women must earn less than men, because they are weaker, they are smaller, they are less intelligent". The worst part is that this is far from being an exception. Today, a growing body of research shows how unconscious bias shapes things like how teachers respond to boys and girls learning math. Gender bias is everywhere. This is the topic of other books but I want to point out that yes, sexism and gender are an issue for mothers, and how we perceive our brain. Perhaps because we, as women, know that we are often not seen as being as smart as men, we are even more conscious of, or sensitive to, the fact that our memory is not working as it should. That could be part of it. There are always many pieces in a puzzle.

Since we're talking about societal pressures, let's touch on culture. Does culture play a role in mommy brain? Is mommy brain just a western culture kind of thing? Again, there doesn't seem to be much research on this. One study[66], carried out on pregnant women living in Kano in northwestern Nigeria, showed that 88.3% of the pregnant women had some sort of mild cognitive impairment. It is not clear exactly what kind of memory or cognitive ability was affected, but this study points to the universality of these effects. Regardless of region or, perhaps, cultural expectations.

Another thing that comes to mind when looking at the research, is how sparse and varied the science is with regards to what mommy brain really is. Overall, based on the meta-analyses I talked about previously, we are seeing slight changes in certain types of memory, but really we need more robust studies on memory in motherhood, i.e.. studies that have hundreds of participants that investigate memory before pregnancy, during pregnancy and in the postpartum. This is called longitudinal research, and it is the best solution to really observe differences in memory across these stages of motherhood. We also need more consistent studies that look at the different types of memory and the components that are important for memory (attention, processing speed, etc.). Memory is complex, and it seems from the studies to date that working memory and verbal memory are the most common areas where moms report having troubles. Knowing where exactly memory deficits may be, or what exactly fogginess is, will help us to better understand mommy brain.

Finally, let's remember that doing a test in the lab and doing a test at home can yield very different results. Remember the study on prospective memory that I did with Prof. Carrie Cuttler? We found that when doing tests in the lab the pregnant women did just as well as the non-pregnant women, but when asked to do something from home (in this case call the lab to confirm their appointment), the pregnant women did much worse than the non-pregnant women. As I mentioned in the previous chapter, we likely will see greater differences in memory when we consider the daily hassles and pressures that exist in the home. When you're in the lab, you can concentrate on the test. When you're at home this isn't always that case. This mental load plays a significant part in our level of brain fog and memory performance in the real world.

## Memory and nesting

If forgetfulness with motherhood does exist, and I believe that it does to some degree (but we need to remember all the amazing things that our mom brain is doing as well), then there must also be a reason for it. Evolutionarily thinking there is an idea that late in pregnancy, when we are rather large and not as mobile, the safest place is to stay is close to home. In doing so, we don't need to use our spatial memory or memory to navigate—which is a type of memory that we see affected in late pregnancy and the early postpartum period in animal models. For example, *the fertility and parental care hypothesis*[67] describes the relatively poor female performance on some spatial memory tasks as serving an adaptive function by decreasing distances traveled from the nest, and thereby increasing female reproductive success[68]. Often, when we think of nesting, we think of birds, but they are not the only ones who nest. In fact, recent research[69] by Dr. Marla Anderson and colleagues at McMaster University in Canada, shows that pregnant women do similar nesting activities as other animals. They prepare a physical space for the baby to live, as well as alter their social environment by limiting who will be present at the time of delivery and who will be visiting in the first days or weeks postpartum.

It is interesting to note that this idea of staying closer to home, and thus modifying one's memory for locations (I talked about this in the previous chapter), makes the best sense if you're a rat. Have you seen a pregnant rat? They can be huge! The average litter is 12 pups but the largest litter I've seen is 26 pups! Imagine if you're a pregnant rat, you'd probably stay close to your nest site and food cache, and avoid wandering through garbage bins. For a rat, it makes sense to have a decrease in spatial memory during late pregnancy, as well as the early postpartum, when you are trying to keep all those pups alive by caring for them—which means licking, nursing, and keeping them warm for a large part of the day. Once the pups are a bit older you can wander about more, but you need to be efficient in your foraging activity to get back to the nest, and protect and care for your young. Efficient foraging relies on improved memory—which is something we see in rats starting about 2 weeks after giving birth, and which lasts past weaning. This increase in spatial memory after weaning, particularly in a first-time mother, may also be to efficiently get out there and find a mate again, but really we're not sure what a rat may be thinking...

## Focusing on what is essential

There exists another reason why the forgetfulness may occur with motherhood. In fact, our ability to think about certain things, or re-member certain things, may be less good, because these things are less important than others. Dr. Donald Winnicott, a famous developmental psychologist, who decades ago spoke of the "good enough" mother, was probably the first to speak of a shift in parental orientation. He called this "primary maternal preoccupation" (what we can probably call today "primary parental preoccupation"), which he defined as "the state immediately after childbirth in which a mother is preoccupied with her child to the exclusion of anything else.[70]" I don't know if it's really true—that we exclude everything else as new mothers—but this idea that we, as parents, are refocusing on the infant makes sense.

Our brains as mothers (and fathers) are focused on caring for the baby and bonding with it. This is where most of our energy is spent. And maybe our brain goes into mommy brain mode to help us refocus on what we need to take care of, which is our baby. In fact, a recent study by Prof. Bridget Callaghan and colleagues[71] at the University of California Los Angeles, shows that pregnant women remember baby-related objects better than non-pregnant women, and have better long-term memory for objects, in general. I think this is an important key to re-framing how we think of mommy brain—there are adaptive changes important for caregiving.

That being said, I really think that the term mommy brain needs a rebrand[72] and should symbolize all the amazing things that our brain is doing to ensure our little one(s) survives. Mommy brain is our brain connecting with our baby and learning how to keep it alive. That's a HUGE deal!

I also think that mommy brain can be a driving force in our ability to take care of ourselves as parents. If we start to think of our brain as something to support and nourish, because of all the work it is doing, maybe we will make friends with the brain fog and forgetfulness, and realize that it is a way for our brain to tell us to slow things down, take a break, or get some support.

True mommy brain is a superpower and I hope we start rebranding it as such. It is a force making us into the parents that we are.

# Part 2
# When the brain becomes pregnant

# Chapter 7.

# Is there a female brain?

Before we look at what is really going on in your mom brain, I think it is important to clarify a few things about the brain and neuroscience research.

## Constant change

Your brain is changing throughout your life. I'm not going to belabor the point here as this seems to be fairly well known now; we can learn new things all life long, even as we age. The word "learning" tells us that our brain changes. The greatest changes in the brain occur during early childhood, but after adolescence the brain isn't hardwired; the connections inside our brain are always being modified. Throughout the years, the adult brain is continually changing in structure and function in response to one's biology, as well as experiences and their environment. In this book, I will talk about brain changes in relation to becoming a parent, a stage in adult life where I believe we are seeing the brain at its most "plastic"—the most modifiable, particularly in a primary caregiver.

## Similar, but different

I remember when, in grad school, my supervisor talked about sex differences in the brain... She used this humorous cartoon drawing of one male brain and one female brain. In the male brain there were large areas designated "sex" and a footnote on the picture stating: "the 'listening to children cry in the middle of the night' gland is not shown due to its small and underdeveloped nature. Best viewed under a microscope". In the female brain there was a large area labelled "need for commitment" and another for "shopping". The area for sex was rather small but overlapped with 'listening'. As you can image, this cartoon drawing was amusing and very stereotypical, but it was obviously not representative of what that science is showing us.

There is no distinct male or female brain. The brain isn't sexually dimorphic. What I mean by "dimorphic" is a characteristic you can find in a specific population (women, for example), and that is completely absent or different in the other population (in men, for example). To illustrate more precisely this dimorphism, the reproductive organs are clearly distinct between males and females in nearly 100% of humans and, more generally, in all mammals. In humans, there are very rare cases where genitalia are ambiguous. And, as far as animals go, female hyenas, to my knowledge, are some of the only animals that don't have sexually dimorphic genitalia. Female hyenas have a penis and they birth via this penis as well. Ouch!

Let's get back to the brain—the brain is not male or female, and it is impossible for anyone, even the most prominent neuroscientist, to determine the brain's sex by looking at it. Though some areas of the brain present some differences (they vary in size, activity, quantity of neurons) between a male and a female, they are not dimorphic.

In *Biopsychology*[73], a text book from my university days, which I brought out again when writing this book, Prof. John Pinel is very clear: "The brains of men and women are alike, but they are not identical." This is what I was taught some years ago. I hope you were taught the same thing, but I'm guessing you may have heard the old dogma that there is a distinct male and female brain, and the reason for this is because of testosterone early in life. Today, we know this isn't true and the situation is much more complex than this. I do want to be clear that it is impossible, when you look at a brain, to say if it belongs to a man or a woman, a male or a female. An analysis of several brains of a male population compared to several brains of a female population will show that, on average, some brain areas are more developed, active or connected in a slightly different way in one sex than the other, but you will need several brains to see these differences. For example, some neurological disorders are more present in women (Alzheimer's disease), and some more present in men (Autism Spectrum Disorder), but this doesn't mean you'll suffer from Alzheimer's disease if you're a woman or you won't be affected by it if you're a man.

## The biggest difference

I was talking to my husband, Prof. Thierry Charlier, about the extent of these sex differences in the brain. He did his doctoral studies investigating the mode of action of steroid hormones in the brain and with sexual behavior, under the supervision of Prof. Jacques Balthazart, who recently wrote *Quand le cerveau devient masculin*[74] (*When the brain becomes male*). Thierry explained to me that, at best, when looking at, for example, different cell populations in the brain, there may be a maximum of a 30% difference between cell populations in a male and a female. This is the case for most mammals, including humans (in very rare examples we know that in some songbird species such as the zebra finch, where the male sings and the female doesn't, some brain regions are clearly more developed in males and almost absent in females. But this is an exception).

When it comes to humans, the number of studies looking at sex and gender differences is small. Most of our data comes from imaging technology, where brain region volumes and blood flow are measured. This last indicator is an easily measurable parameter that allows for the estimation of the activity of a brain region. That being said, these parameters are relatively imprecise compared to the accuracy we can obtain by using animal models. Thus, in humans, we rarely know what is going on at the level of a hormone or neurotransmitter. This prevents us from studying the subtler differences between the sexes. However, these studies show clearly that there are a number of differences in the structure and the functioning of the brain in men and women. Note—I've written differences, not dimorphisms!

These differences observed between men and women are partly due to an exposure to testosterone during development, at birth and during puberty. But it's not the only factor responsible for these effects.[75] There are a number of biological factors implicated in sexual differentiation of the brain and behavior. The bottom line is that the brain of a male or female—a man, a woman, a LGBTQ+ person—is similar in many ways BUT there are differences.[76] It's also not the entire brain that is different between males and females (or with gender), but some regions in one individual may be different compared to some regions of the opposite sex (or another gender). In addition, in the same individual, some brain regions can present male characteristics, while other brain regions, in the same individual, don't show this sexualization. It is generally only at the level of a population that we can say a brain region is more developed in males (it's the case, for instance, in certain neurons in the brain area called the bed nucleus of the stria terminalis), or more developed in in females (for instance, in certain neurons in the infundibular region of the brain).

In addition to this, humans have genders, a social definition added to the biological component (the sex, XX or XY). That is why some researchers have proposed that we should be thinking of the human brain as a mosaic—a sum of the parts, and perhaps less as a blend.[77] Generally speaking, this idea makes sense to me because research on sex differences in the brain supports this idea. The differences between what we may call a male or female brain are nuanced, but that's not to say that there are not sex differences in the brain. There are. They are subtle, influenced by our biology, but also the culture and environment we're evolving in, and can significantly impact behavior.

In this book, I will probably speak of the female or maternal brain, or male or paternal brain; and I mean to do this in a sense that the brain is slightly more male-like or slightly more female-like, not that it is distinct as male or female.

## Sexist science

In addition to this idea of a male or female brain, science has been sexist, for lack of a better word, for some time. Sure, there are many of us who understand the importance of sex in neuroscience, biomedical research and medicine, but not as many who don't see the importance. The majority of neuroscience research is done in males, probably for many reasons, but one being that females are "complicated" by hormones. I hear this excuse from both men and women scientists. Shocking, I know.

Recently the narrative of neuroscience and sex has started to change. With Prof. Christina Dalla and Dr. Nikos Kokras, colleagues at the National and Kapodistrian University of Athens, Greece, as well as my husband, we recently published an article in a special issue[78] on sex differences in neuroscience and neuropharmacology in the *European Journal of Neuroscience* where we wrote that "a greater focus on sex differences and women's health is needed in European, as well as worldwide, neuroscience research." Perhaps that's an understatement, given the gaps in our understanding of the link between sex, gender, and our brains, but I hope we continue to see more research in this area.

On a positive note, policies are changing. In 2015, policies of different funding and health care agencies [the National Institutes of Health[79] (NIH, USA NOT-OD-15-102), the Canadian Institutes of Health Research (CIHR/IRSC), Natural Sciences and Engineering Research Council of Canada (NSERC/CRSNG) and European Union policy for Horizon 2020 programs (2016)] urged the incorporation of both male and female subjects in all funded research projects, with the aim of improving our understanding of sex-specific effects in health and disease. This is a move in the right direction. I would take this need for studying sex and gender one step further to consider the impact of reproduction and parenting on our brains.

What about the parental brain? Are mom brains and dad brains really sexually differentiated? Yes and no. It's largely a question of experience with a child (more in Part 3), but it's probably impacted by the relationship between the parents (if there are two parents), as well as many biological and environmental factors influencing this difference. We are a complex species.

Chapter 8.

# A mother's love

I'm not going to lie—I'm one of those moms who instantly fell in love with her newborn. I posted on my Facebook page that "She is the most adorable baby ever!!! And it was definitely the best day of our lives!". It still is. The fact that I produced a human still blows my mind— and I produced two!

But what made me fall in love with her? I think I was in the right place at the right time, and my brain was primed and ready to go. I was lucky. This isn't always the case, and it was different with my second (less impactful). We're all different and our parenting journey is too.

## Is it instinct?

The dreaded "maternal instinct"; this idea that you know what you're doing when you have a baby. You don't. Prof. Alison Fleming, a pioneer in the field of maternal brain research, said it best when she said[80] "it's not like there's an instinct called mothering... It's just a matter of getting the experience and the interaction... There are many ways to get to the same end". Exactly. There are many ways to mother.

There is no switch that turns on, when you birth a baby, that allows you to know what you should be doing. It's a process of trial and error. However, I do believe that birthing parents often have a greater drive to care for their baby, based on hormonal cues priming their brain to rapidly learn to respond to, and care for, their baby. But, anyone can parent, not just birthing mothers.

# What is Mother Love?

When we think of motherhood, we think of love—usually unconditional love for your child or children. It makes sense biologically to love your child, to care for them, but what does this mean in terms of the brain.

Love is defined in the Oxford dictionary[81] as "an intense feeling of deep affection and a great interest and pleasure in something. A feeling or disposition of deep affection or fondness for someone, typically arising from a recognition of attractive qualities, from natural affinity, or from sympathy and manifesting itself in concern for the other's welfare and pleasure in his or her presence". It is often something we talk about when we talk about our children. Generally, we love them. What love is, exactly, is perhaps a discussion for another book.

When it comes to mother love, we know that it is often idealized. However, if you've read *L'amour en plus*[82] (*Mother Love* in English) by Elizabeth Badinter, you will start to realize that mothers don't necessarily "love" their children. This may be due to the fact that we are all different and when given choices (for example, about childcare), these differences are more evident. This may also be due to the fact that mother love can be affected by society and culture, something we see throughout history, but something that still exists today. Internal and external factors affect who we are and how we mother.

In her book titled *Mother Nature*[83], Prof. Sarah Blaffer Hrdy gives an additional account of what it is to be a mother. She points out the range of maternal behaviors that exist in mothers from traditional (hunter-gatherer) and more modern societies. There is a huge range of what is 'natural'—from not wanting a child to adoring it. But one thing that seems to be important is interacting with a newborn. Experience with your infant matters (something I'm sure I'll repeat a million times in this book).

## The brain on love

We know there are brain areas that are activated with love. Research on this topic has primarily focused on romantic love, but one study[84] has identified and compared brain regions that are involved in two types of love; romantic or friendship love and maternal love.

One of the premises of this study was that romantic and maternal love have a common evolutionary purpose, which is the maintenance and perpetuation of the species. Both these types of love or attachments (the two words are constantly interchangeable throughout the article) are based on forming a bond with someone else; which implies that being with this person is rewarding. We also know that hormones, primarily oxytocin, play an important role in these relationships. Thus, it would make sense that there are common brain areas activated by these hormones when we are with someone we love.

The study of Bartels and Zeki consisted of 20 mothers as participants. The researchers asked them to provide a photo of their own child, a photo of another child of the same age with whom they had been acquainted for the same length of time, a photo of their best friend and a photo of another person they were acquainted with. I think it would have made better sense to provide a picture of their partner or husband but maybe the throes of parenting altered the romantic love for their significant other.

While mothers were viewing the different photos, measurements of brain activity took place with fMRI (functional magnetic resonance imaging) brain scanning techniques, where brain activity is measured by detecting blood flow. After this, each mother was asked to rate the intensity of her feelings during the scan for each of the children and adults viewed. The results obtained from this study were compared with other results of the same laboratory[85] which focused on how romantic love activated the brain. From these two sets of results, the researchers found that:

1. Romantic or friendship and maternal love both involve an overlapping set of brain areas, as well as brain areas that are specific to each.

2. The activated brain areas belong to the reward system, and are also known to contain a high density of receptors for oxytocin and vasopressin. Suggesting that the neurohormonal control of these strong forms of attachment observed in animals also applies to humans.

3. Both forms of attachment (friendship and motherhood) suppressed activity in brain regions associated with negative emotions, as well as brain regions associated with "mentalizing" and social judgment.

The authors concluded that attachment processes employ a push-pull mechanism that activates one brain network—related to reward—while deactivating another—related to negative emotions. The authors conclude that this push-pull mechanism explains "the power of love to motivate and exhilarate". I'm not sure I'd go that far in my interpretation of the research findings, but knowing that love has a place in the brain is an interesting concept.

## The neural network of parenthood

When we, as neuroscientists, talk about parenting and the brain we generally don't talk about love. We talk about things that are likely components of love: motivation, empathy, reward, to name a few. Think about your baby if you have one: you're probably more motivated to care for your baby than another baby, right? You're also more likely to think your baby is the cutest ever (a sign of finding him/her rewarding), no? I certainly did. When my kids were babies they were the cutest ever. These are just a couple of examples of the components of love.

When it comes to research on the maternal brain (more commonly called "parental brain research" because of the similarities in the brain areas in moms, dads and parents), we often talk about the parental care-giving network. It consists of a number of interconnected brain areas that work together to coordinate responses to an infant, through a trial and error process of learning.

Much of the research on the parental brain, which has focused on mothers, has been done in animal models (as previously mentioned) but the research in humans often parallels and expands these findings in animals.

Prof. Ruther Feldman, a leader in the field of parental brain research in humans, sums up the components of the global parental care-giving network nicely in a review article published in 2015[86]. Brain changes with motherhood exist in subcortical brain circuits that we share with other mammals, which include regions such as the hypothalamus, amygdala, ventral tegmental area, nucleus accumbens and ventral pallidum. These brain areas are important for things like anxiety, motivation and reward, to name a few. We also see a number of changes in brain cortical circuits in humans that involve more sophisticated mental functions, important for parenting, such as empathy, mentalizing or the ability to figure out what someone needs, and emotional regulation[87]. In her review, Prof. Feldman points out one important difference in the human parental brain: the human parental caregiving network involves connecting a number of the subcortical brain structures to multiple insula-cingulate and frontal temporoparietal networks. That is, the human parental brain consists of integrating more cortical brain areas, likely due to the fact that we have a more highly developed cortex that mediates more complex behaviors than other mammals.

## Master mind

If you think about it, the parental brain is a master system using brain networks mediating complex behaviors in order to appropriately care for a baby—to keep a human alive. In other words, you become a master mind reader and, perhaps, a *mama bear.*

In fact, the maternal brain has been proposed to be the basis of attachment. When I spoke with Prof. Larry Young, from Emory University, on my podcast *Mommy Brain Revisited*[88] about his ground-breaking research on oxytocin and bonding, he said that "the evolutionary origin of empathy is in the maternal brain". Imagine that. The network of the maternal brain is the origin of empathy; a key component of how we form relationships. That is a powerful concept!

## Nature and nurture

There are likely a number of physiological events, mainly hormonal changes, during pregnancy, birth and postpartum, that play a role in activating the parental brain network. These hormones likely have a more rapid impact on the parental brain network in birthing parents, but hormones also play a role in non-birthing parents (refer to Chapter 13).

In addition to these physiological factors, we need to keep in mind that our brains are incredibly plastic and affected by internal *and* external cues. Thus, the context in which we mother or parent is dependent on our biology and environment. There are fundamental changes in the brain that occur with pregnancy and birth but when we look at the development of the parental brain, we are starting to see the importance of environmental factors, such as stress. I suspect that culture, religion, and gender also play a role. Nature and nurture always interact.

## The importance of mother love

If you asked me, as a daughter, how I know my mother loves me, I would say it's in a million little things and some big things too. It's a feeling, but there is biology backing it up. It's a large part of why I am "me".

I've heard it said that "mothering begets mothering", and I hope in my case that it's true.

Chapter 9.

# Brain shrinkage with motherhood?

When I was in grad school, I read a scientific paper[89] that said "the female brain is the pinnacle of neural development, and it is an exemplar of evolution's relentless march toward perfection." The feminist in me won't disagree with this statement, but then it went on to say, "The female brain, however, as remarkable as it is, does not reach fruition, its maximal capacity if you will, unless and until it engages in the complex set of behaviors for which it was designed, and from which it derives its most important benefits: reproduction and, in the case of many species, care and protection of the young." This I have a problem with. Of course, I think the maternal brain is pretty amazing but I don't think it is the destiny of women to be mothers. Your brain is not any less amazing if you do not parent a child. I want to make that clear. But your brain does change when you are pregnant and mother a child. That is something that is important to understand. It changes in many ways and overall, this is a good thing.

## Fine tuning the system

How does your brain change when you become a mom? I'm guessing you've heard that your brain shrinks. That's been a bit of a hot topic lately, and also a reason that has been used as to why being a mom is so hard: your brain is just not functioning, it's smaller. However, that's not really true. Being a mom is challenging, but it's not because your brain is shrinking—it's likely due to a number of societal issues (beyond the scope of this book). We live in a patriarchal society after all, and although things are changing for women, they aren't changing fast enough.

You know that saying *dynamite comes in small packages*? Sometimes I think that applies to your mom brain. Less can be more. In fact, *less can be more* is part of the title of a review on the maternal brain that I recently wrote with other experts in the field[90]. I'll sum up some key points from our review below.

The first study on brain structural changes across pregnancy in women was published in 2002[91]. This study wasn't the most robust study carried out on the maternal brain (with sometimes only two women having their brains imaged at a given time point), but it did provide the first brain images of women prior to conception, during pregnancy, and after delivery. The researchers showed that there was a reduction in overall brain size in women during pregnancy. This decrease in brain size was about 5% from preconception to birth. Not a huge change, but a significant one. They also showed that by 20 weeks postpartum the brain returned back to its preconception size. I'm not sure how this research finding was accepted at the time, and I couldn't find any press articles about it, but I think it's an important discovery. To show that the adult brain shrinks across pregnancy is something remarkable.

As I said, this study was done on only a few women so further research was needed. Unfortunately, it wasn't for 15 years that further research took place! In 2017, Dr. Elseline Hoekzema and colleagues[92], then part of Dr. Susanna Carmona's group at the University of Madrid, investigated how the brain changes in volume across pregnancy, but they looked in detail at specific brain regions—because your brain is essentially the sum of many different parts—each with a significant role to play in the control of different emotions and behaviors. For example, they looked at changes in the volume of the amygdala, a brain area important for emotional regulation, among other things; changes in the volume of cortical areas important for decision making; and changes in the brain area of the hippocampus, important for stress regulation and memory. The researchers also investigated how attached a mother felt toward her baby, in order to understand how changes in the volume of different brain areas may be related to being a mother.

The study focused on grey matter volume changes[93] in a number of brain areas and compared 25 moms with 20 non-moms (they also included dads and non-dads but found no differences between the two groups in the measurements they looked at). The women participated in a session of brain imaging (MRI) before becoming pregnant, and within days or weeks of giving birth. Elseline and her colleagues showed that mothers undergo "extensive and highly consistent" reductions in regional grey matter volumes across pregnancy (from pre-pregnancy to shortly after birth). Changes that remain for at least 2 years after delivery (and even up to 6 years)[94], except in the hippocampus, where the size increased in the postpartum period but did not return to pre-conception size.

When looking in more detail at these brain changes, they found that the brain areas that decreased in volume (the medial frontal cortex, precuneus, posterior cingulate cortex, inferior frontal gyri[95] and superior temporal sulci) overlapped with the neural network regulating *Theory of Mind,* or the ability to understand someone's intentions and emotions; this is something incredibly important when you're taking care of a baby! In addition, these decreases in brain region volumes predicted increased feelings of attachment by a mother for her baby early in the postpartum period (and they didn't relate to memory, at least on the memory tests used in this study). In summary, essentially *less is more,* or, as I like to think about it, there is a fine tuning of the female brain across pregnancy and birth—at least in terms of brain size. This is a good thing and that is pretty cool.

## All is not lost

I just talked about brain structure changes across pregnancy but what about during the postpartum period when so much learning and interacting with baby is going on? As I mentioned above, many of the brain areas showing a decrease in volume remain smaller up to 6 years postpartum, but it seems, from the research of others, that there are times during the postpartum period when there is an increase in brain region volumes, perhaps corresponding to parenting. For one thing, white matter[96] volume increases during the postpartum period[97], indicating that more than just neurons are being changed. And when it comes to grey matter volume in the early weeks or months postpartum, studies show that there are increases in grey matter volume in a number of cortical and subcortical areas in new mothers[98]. Many of these brain areas are the same brain areas shown to decrease in size after pregnancy. This suggests to me that during the early postpartum months, when you are learning to parent, the brain is adjusting to learning these new skills, and this is why we may see an increase in cortical thickness in particular brain regions, such as the prefrontal cortex, important for decision making, and the lateral occipital cortex, a brain area important for recognition[99]. This is at least one idea and more research is needed to understand the time course of these brain changes during the first weeks and months postpartum.

What is indisputable is that the brain changes during pregnancy and across the postpartum period. These changes are significant and normal. They are often seen as a reduction in brain volume in many brain areas, but this reduction is associated with improvements in parenting. Less is more.

I've known Elseline for a few years now, as I've organized that we give talks together at a few conferences[100]. I've also had her on my podcast[101] to talk about the effects of pregnancy on the brain. One thing that I love about her is how devoted she is to understanding the maternal brain; how curious she is about it and the amazing work she is doing in women to understand these brain changes. I also love that her data points to something remarkable in brain imaging and that is the consistency of the effects of pregnancy on the brain. She recently told me: "The effects of pregnancy on the brain are so consistent that women can be classified as having been pregnant based on the images of their brain." That, I think, is amazing. Pregnancy imprints on your brain.

## Under the microscope

In some ways, I'm not surprised that the brain imaging data is pointing to such pronounced effects on the structure of the maternal brain in women; we've seen many changes in the maternal brain in animal models over the years. Some of these changes are similar and some are different than what are seen in women. In animal models, the advantage is that we can examine more precisely the changes that are occurring in the brain. These models allow us to look beyond volume differences, to differences in, for example, the number or structure of neurons or glial cells, the primary building blocks of the brain.

That is what I did for my doctoral thesis, I looked at how motherhood affected the production of new neurons (neurogenesis) in the hippocampus—a brain area important for memory and the regulation of stress, and one that is also affected by hormones. I found that in new mother rats there is a reduction in the number of new neurons being produced in the hippocampus[102]. At the time, this was counterintuitive because it was assumed that neurogenesis would increase with motherhood due to the changes in hormones and the learning that takes place. But this isn't what we found. Other researchers[103] have reported similar findings of a decrease in neurogenesis in the hippocampus, as well as the amygdala, of mothers. This is perhaps another level of fine tuning the maternal brain. This result agrees with what was shown in human mothers, and allows us to understand, at a cellular level, what may be responsible for some of the structural changes.

I've recently shown that the number of new neurons in the hippocampus decreases in late pregnancy as well; it isn't just birth that is initiating these changes[104]. The brain seems to be fine tuning throughout pregnancy in preparation for motherhood. We don't know exactly what this decrease in new neurons in the hippocampus means in terms of function—likely it is related to changes in memory or stress regulation—but what I am talking about here is the fact that there are structural changes that are occurring at many levels in the maternal brain. We also see a decrease in microglia cells during pregnancy and the postpartum period[105]. These cells are related to immune function and likely play a very important role in the maternal brain[106], with recent research suggesting they have a role in maternal behavior. We'll talk more about functional brain changes in the coming sections, but overall what we are seeing is a number of changes in the maternal brain from volume of the overall brain to number of neurons and microglial cells, and even to changes in the density of receptors that are necessary and healthy for mothering to take place.

## Across species

This fine tuning of the brain isn't just found in humans or rodents. We see it in other species as well, which suggests that it is highly conserved. However, it can be different depending on what's being studied and in what animal.

Let's talk about sheep for a minute. I love sheep and have a few of my own (five Ouessant sheep)—and ewes are pretty amazing. Ours gave birth in the spring and I was fortunate to be there for one of the births. It's incredible how everything just works with birth and how the ewe is responsive to the cues from the lamb... When talking about studying the brains of ewes, the researchers that come to mind, for me, are those at the INRAE[107] in Nouzilly—Dr. Frederic Levy and Dr. Matthieu Keller. I met Fred years ago when I was doing my Master's in Toronto. He is a longtime collaborator of Prof. Alison Fleming and was visiting her in Toronto the year that I was there. I had a chance to visit Fred's lab in Nouzilly in 2008 and spent an early morning in the barn with the sheep helping with one of their studies investigating hormonal regulation of maternal recognition of her young at the time of birth. It was a great experience.

Over the past decade or so, Fred and Matthieu have looked at neurogenesis in the brain of ewes to determine whether it changes and how. Specifically, they looked at the production of new neurons in the hippocampus, as well as the olfactory bulb of sheep mothers. They found[108] that, in both of these brain areas, there is a reduction in the number of new neurons, similar to what is seen in the rodent hippocampus (but opposite to what is seen in the rodent olfactory bulb[109]), and they showed that these new neurons are important for mothering. Thus, there is a conserved effect of certain brain changes with motherhood. However, some changes likely differ based on the species studied. We are all similar, but we are also different.

Besides mammals, we know that in many avian species the brain changes in size with the breeding season. Even in invertebrates recent research in ants (*Harpegnathos saltator*) shows that a female ant's brain size prior to laying eggs decreases by 24% in the optic lobes[110]. Imagine that! That's huge. It's thought that this decrease in an ant's brain size with reproduction is important to divert energy resources to egg laying, and is associated with changes in reproductive hormone concentrations. More research is needed on this, but I love that even in ants the brain is *fine tuning* with reproduction.

## More than meets the eye

Many of the brain changes are decreases (or what I like to call fine tuning of the brain), but many changes are increases too. For example, in rodent mothers, we see an increase in neurogenesis in the olfactory bulbs, and also an increase in the neural complexity (as the number of synapses) in the MPOA[111], a brain area impacting a number of behavioral processes. In addition, recent work in mice by Dr. Matthieu Keller's group[112], mentioned above, shows that grey matter volumes across pregnancy and the postpartum period actually increase, and don't decrease with motherhood. This research is a beautiful example of just how 'plastic' the maternal brain is. Their article is open access[113], so I'd encourage you to take a look at their supplemental material to see the video of brain changes across pregnancy in female mice, as compared to non-pregnant counterparts. It's very interesting!

I could continue to describe the data with regards to structural changes in the maternal brain, but I think I will leave it there as I'm hoping these examples show that the brain changes structurally on many levels with pregnancy and motherhood. This is normal and is related to being able to care for your child.

## How great is the change?

You've probably heard the term "matrescence" but let's review it here. "Matrescence" is a term coined by an American anthropologist, Dr. Dana Raphael. It is "the time of mother-becoming[114]." This is a period when there are physical, psychological and emotional transformations. It's a significant stage in a female's lifespan, although, unlike adolescence, we don't all become mothers.

If we think of matrescence as a kind of adult adolescence, what does this mean in terms of the magnitude of brain changes? I think we can all accept that adolescence is a time in life when the brain changes significantly. We have the data to prove that. Not only is the brain changing with adolescence, but hormones are "all over the place" and there are a number of changes physiologically as well. It's a major life event, and so is motherhood.

Can the brain changes during matrescence compare to changes during adolescence? I mentioned above, that in the first study on brain structural changes in women across pregnancy, where they had very few women participating in the study, they showed about a 5% decrease in overall brain size across pregnancy. The more recent research led by Elseline and her team in a larger group of women (25) shows that there is a 1% decrease in size of different brain areas. This is significant but in the grand scheme of things, 1% of anything is really quite small.

In 2019, Dr. Susanna Carmona, Dr. Elseline Hoekzema and colleagues, did a study to better understand how matrescence and adolescence may compare in terms of brain changes[115]. To do this, they examined cortical thickness and how it may differ between first-time moms, adolescent girls, and adult women who had never been mothers. The results of this study showed that cortical thickness measurements in moms and adolescent girls were almost identical, and they were significantly different from adult women who had never been mothers. They showed there is cortical flattening in moms and adolescent girls—again pointing to this idea of "fine tuning" the maternal brain. They speculated that hormonal changes with matrescence and adolescence may be the reason for these brain changes, but further research is needed to make this link.

The point here is that the changes in brain size with motherhood are as significant as changes in brain size with adolescence. Motherhood is a life event, a developmental stage that changes the female brain.

# Chapter 10

# The whole is greater than the sum of the parts[116]

I read recently that if size mattered the elephant would be the king of the jungle, but then again "of course size matters, no one wants a small glass of wine" (original source unknown). So maybe size does matter, sometimes. But when we talk about the parental brain, it's brain size AND function that are important.

Brain function in the context of the human brain is usually measured as brain activity by fMRI (functional magnetic resonance imaging) or EEG (electroencephalogram) techniques. fMRI measures brain activity by detecting changes associated with blood flow throughout the brain in response to a cue (i.e. picture or sound) or at rest (i.e. resting state). The part of your brain that functions is going to need more energy which is provided by increased blood flow. EEG is a method to record electrical activity of the brain via electrodes fixed on the scalp. This electrical activity represents macroscopic activity of the surface layer of the brain.

It is important to note, that brain function not only includes the function of neurons, but also connections between neurons and neurochemicals that allow neurons to communicate, glial cells, and a number of other factors that make up the core of how the brain works. Our understanding of this deeper level of brain functioning is primarily from research in animal models. This research in animal models shows that there is an intricate interplay between a number of these neural factors that mediate parental care-giving behaviors, that allow us to better understand the neurobiology of these behaviors, and which can help us envision in more detail what is occurring in the human brain. But here I will focus on what we know about studies on human brain function with parenting.

## The first step

Brain imaging techniques are relatively new, especially in the context of parental brain research. It wasn't until 1999, just 20 or so years ago, that Dr. Jeffrey Lorberbaum and his colleagues used fMRI to study how brain activity may change with motherhood. This first study[117] was relatively simple; the brains of mothers were observed while they were listening to an infant cry. It may seem obvious that the brain is activated when a baby is crying (how could it not be?), but of course this first step needed to be taken.

This pioneering study examined the brain of four mothers whose children were between three weeks and 3.5 years of age. This is a rather small cohort of mothers with a rather large age range of children—not ideal for research, but the science needed to start somewhere. The activity of the brains of these mothers was measured while they were listening to the sound of an infant crying or to white noise. The researchers discovered (surprise, surprise!) that compared to white noise, listening to an infant cry activated brain regions involved in processing new and rewarding stimuli, such as the anterior cingulate cortex (ACC) and the right orbitofrontal cortex (OFC). This was the first study to show that a mother's brain responds to infant cry in a different way than to noise in general. This was ground-breaking research that paved the way for further studies of the human parental brain.

## The gestating brain

Since this time a number of studies using neuroimaging and EEG have been done to understand how the brain changes with motherhood. Studies during pregnancy are few and are often limited to EEG research due to a concern that fMRI measurements are not ideal for pregnant women (however, this idea is changing).

The studies using EEG to measure brain activation or "brain waves" during pregnancy show that the brain adapts and prepares for motherhood. A large portion of this research has concentrated on social cognition, that's to say the way that we process, remember and use information to explain and predict the behavior of others. This aspect is very important when one has a baby, as it is essential to understand the needs of the baby, but also to recognize risky and safe places, in order to provide a safe environment for the baby.

Recent studies show that while looking at photos of an emotional or fearful face (for example, an angry face) pregnant women have differences in brain activation in prefrontal brain areas compared to non-pregnant women[118, 119]. These changes in brain activation parallel research showing that during pregnancy women are better at recognizing faces[120], better at recognizing threatening faces[121] and prefer individuals perceived as healthier[122]. I bet you didn't know that your brain was doing these things when you were pregnant, did you?

Besides these changes in how the brain processes social cues during pregnancy, recent research has started to look at whether brain activity during pregnancy is associated with caring for a baby[123]. One of my favorite studies on this topic, and the first of its kind, was carried out at the University of Toronto (where I did my MA) by Dr. Joanna Dudek and her colleagues in 2020[124]. It aimed to investigate if brain cortical activation in response to photos of a baby during late pregnancy could be related to a mother's feeling of attachment to her baby after birth. Forty mothers participated in the study (28 were first-time mothers). They visited the lab once during the third trimester and once at 3-5 months after birth. During the laboratory visits, EEG measurements were done while they were looking at a series of different pictures of infant or adult faces. At the postpartum visit, the mothers were asked to fill out a questionnaire about mother-infant bonding (the *Postpartum Bonding Questionnaire*). The study found that prenatal to postnatal increases in certain measurements of brain cortical activity while viewing infant faces predicted a stronger bond between the mother and her own infant in the postpartum. This is exciting research and points to how changes in the brain during pregnancy may prepare the maternal brain to care for a baby.

## Preference for your own baby

Over the past 20 years, most of the research on the human parental brain (which hasn't been extensive) has used fMRI techniques and focused on the postpartum period. This approach is more expensive and more difficult to set up than EEG, but it makes it possible to observe all the regions of the brain, and not just brain activity near the scalp, as in the case of EEG. These studies using fMRI have investigated how different areas of a mother's brain react to infant-related cues such as photos, sounds (i.e. cries), movies, and smell (don't you just love that baby smell!)[125]. In many of these studies, which often use photos, maternal brain activity was investigated as a mother looked at a photo of her infant, a photo of a stranger's infant or a non-infant photo (an adult or nature scene used as a control). The majority of this research shows that a mother displays greater brain activation in response to a cue from her own infant compared to another infant[126], showing a preference for her own child.

Maternal brain areas consistently activated in response to cues of her own versus other infant, as observed in systematic literature reviews or meta-analyses, include the insula, orbitofrontal gyrus, inferior frontal gyrus, precentral gyrus, thalamus, amygdala, hypothalamus and striatum[127]. These brain regions are active in several neural networks mediating aspects of parental care-giving behaviors such as reward, empathy and emotional regulation.

## Motivation and reward

As I mentioned previously, finding a baby rewarding is one of the most important components of parenting. If we find an infant rewarding we will be motivated to care for them. Research in animal models has shown that there are significant changes to the brain's reward circuitry with motherhood, and these changes play a crucial role in a mother's motivation to care for her young[128]. The core brain areas important for reward include the nucleus accumbens, amygdala, hippocampus and various prefrontal brain areas.

Research on the human maternal brain has shown that when viewing or hearing their infants, many of these reward-related brain regions in mothers are also activated. One recent study, led by Dr. Shir Atzil and their colleagues[129], has gone one step further to show that dopamine levels (dopamine being the primary neurotransmitter involved in reward processing) in the brain of human mothers is related to maternal care-giving behavior. This groundbreaking study used an additional neuro-imaging technique called positron emission tomography (PET—where neurochemical changes can also be investigated by using a radioactive tracer to look at metabolic activity of a specific neurochemical of interest) coupled with fMRI techniques, to investigate the activity of dopamine and the connectivity of key components of the reward circuitry in re-sponse to viewing a video of her infant or an unfamiliar infant. In ad-dition, the synchrony between the mothers and their infants was assessed while they were interacting. This behavioral synchrony, par-ticularly vocalizations such as motherese, was used as a measure of bonding.

The main findings from this study show that the stronger the mother-infant bond, the greater the dopamine response in the brain areas es-sential for reward, such as the nucleus accumbens. They also found that maternal-infant bonding is associated with increased connectivity be-tween the nucleus accumbens, the amygdala and the medial prefrontal cortex—key components of the parental brain. This study showed that in addition to the literature on oxytocin and bonding in humans[130], brain dopamine levels may be key to forming bonds, not only between a mother and a child, but also in relationships, in general. You need more than oxytocin to bond to your baby.

## Empathy

Another key component of being a parent and mother is to be able to be empathic, but also be able to understand what baby may need (that's what we call the Theory of Mind, mentioned above). In the brain, the anterior insula and anterior cingulate cortex play crucial roles in empa-thy, while the theory of mind network includes various brain midline areas such as the precuneus, posterior cingulate and medial frontal cortex, as well as the anterior temporal lobes, temporo-parietal junction, superior temporal sulcus and inferior frontal gyri. These brain areas are highly activated in mothers when they are presented with cues from their infants, and a recent meta-analysis of this research showed that mothers have even stronger brain activity when viewing their own infant as opposed to someone else's infant in brain areas such as the insula, inferior frontal gyrus, basal ganglia and thalamus[131]. It still remains to be determined what neurochemicals are involved in empathy in motherhood, but it is clear that the ability to care for, and respond to, baby is specifically wired in the brain.

## Emotional regulation

The ability to detect and respond appropriately to a baby is a large part of parenting. It takes time to get it right and is likely a dynamic process that changes with experience and the development of the child. Two brain networks are known for processing and responding to information. These are the salience network and the emotion regulation network. The salience network, which is built around paralimbic brain structures such as the dorsal anterior cingulate and orbital fronto-insular cortices, is activated in response to highly salient and relevant stimuli, resulting in a state of alertness. The emotion regulation network, which comprises of many brain areas including those in the prefrontal cortex and the amygdala, provides the ability to modulate the trajectory of an emotion. Research is beginning to show that these networks are activated in the maternal brain primarily when viewing one's own, versus an unfamiliar, infant[132], and especially if the cue is a negative emotional cue signaling infant distress, such as crying[133]. This makes sense as distress indicates danger or threat and the desire to keep your baby alive is generally quite high. Thus, a mother, and parent, uses these brain networks to detect the cue (salience network) and respond appropriately to it (emotional regulation).

## Key regulator

The activity of the hypothalamus is also affected by motherhood. The hypothalamus is an ancient brain area that is found in all vertebrates, which has been well conserved across evolution and is essential for maintaining homeostasis of the body by controlling the release and reception of hormones necessary for mating, pregnancy, birth, and suckling; such as oxytocin, prolactin, progesterone and estrogen, among others. The activation of this brain region increases when a mother looks at a photo of her infant, which seems logical as this is the "seat" of so many hormones important for maternal care, and life in general. This brain region is also implicated in other regulatory processes (hunger, drinking, thermal regulation...). We wouldn't survive if we didn't have our hypothalamus.

## Links with maternal care?

If different brain areas are activated in response to infant cues, does that have anything to do with how a mother feels about her baby? The short answer is yes! Although we can't manipulate a mother-infant relationship in human research as we can with animal models, a few neuroimaging studies in mothers have investigated the link between a mother's brain activity to an infant cue (usually crying) with the mother-infant relationship (as briefly mentioned above with dopamine). These studies show that a mother's brain activation patterns to the sound of her infant crying are related to how attached she is to her infant[134] and how sensitive she is to her infant's needs[135].

Other research shows that across the postpartum period, and with parenting experience, brain activity changes in key areas important for processing emotions[136]. It seems the longer time one spends being a mother is associated with greater infant-specific activity in key parental brain regions, such as the orbitofrontal cortex and the amygdala. But more than that, this research speaks to the importance of experience, and how parenting is an adaptive dynamic process for behavior and for the brain.

## Is it just about baby?

What happens to the maternal brain if there are no infant cues (no photo of the baby for example)? Studies have recently aimed to answer this question by looking at brain activity when a mom is "at rest" using fMRI. This research shows that a mother's brain activity at rest is different than a woman's who hasn't mothered—particularly in frontal, parietal, and limbic regions[137], areas important for empathy and theory of mind. Other research has shown that brain activation and connectivity at rest differs across the postpartum period, particularly in brain regions of the salience network and motivation system[138]. This shows, again, the impact of experience on the ever-changing parental brain.

Chapter 11.

# The second time around?

I often get asked, what about the second time, or the third or fourth: how does having more kids affect the brain? The short answer is we don't know much, at least in the early years postpartum period. We do know that with aging, the number of kids you have can have an effect on your brain (see the following chapter for more details).

From personal experience, I can tell you that the first time is much different than the second. This is likely because it is the first time—the first time caring for a baby—so there are many things to be learned. In some ways, this experience of the first time helps the second time, but then again, the second time you have two kids, so that experience is new too.

## Memory for motherhood

It is generally considered that when you become a mother (and likely a parent) this is a time when "maternal memory" occurs in the brain[139]. This is a memory of how to respond and care for a newborn. Profs Bob Bridges and Alison Fleming, pioneers in the field of maternal brain research, did the foundational studies on this subject, and showed that experience in mothering leads to more efficient expressions of maternal care, modulated by a number of changes in the brain. The key here is that experience in mothering is necessary.

Maternal memory makes sense. Research in human mothers shows that an experienced mom recognizes and interprets a baby's crying better and faster than a first-time mom[140]. They also rate infants' cries as less piercing[141].

Most of the research on the human parental brain in mothers and fathers has been done in first-time parents—probably because we would anticipate seeing the greatest changes in the brain with the first experience and because it's much easier to get first-time parents into the lab, as they only have one child to care for.

As mentioned previously, I did my doctoral thesis on the question of how maternal experience affects the hippocampus—a brain area important for memory, stress regulation and affected by steroid hormones. In brief, my research in mother rats showed that, when looking at the production of new neurons in the hippocampus, first-time mother rats[142] showed more pronounced changes in the number of new neurons compared to age-matched second-time mothers. Second-time mothers still showed some changes compared to never mothered rats, just not to the same extent as the first-time mothers. Further research in animal models, although sparse, also speaks to this effect of maternal experience on maternal brain plasticity.

## The first time is the worst time?

But what about the effect of having had two or more children on the maternal brain in women? There really isn't much research on this—at most two studies, and only one with a large enough group size to be worth talking about. This study[143], out of Dr. Helena Rutherford's lab at Yale, looked at how brain event-related potentials (a type of "brain wave") in mothers was affected by viewing photos of an unfamiliar infant that was happy, sad, or neutral, and listening to high- and low-distress cries from an unfamiliar infant. The study found that having previously had children modulated the postpartum brain response most notably to infant cries. The authors conclude that first-time mothers have enhanced neural responses to auditory and visual infant cues. This suggests that first-time mothers have increased attention to emotional cues of the infant compared to experienced mothers.

This finding of reproductive experience effects on brain activity makes sense to me. As a first time parent, everything about the baby is new and you are figuring out (i.e. learning) what to do and how to respond to infant cues. The second time, your brain recognizes these situations and already has learned some ways to respond to baby and is less "surprised". It has less learning to do.

## Practice makes perfect?

Our brain learns to adapt to a baby the first time, and once it has parented one time, there is a memory of this experience that can be beneficial the second time and likely all the times afterward.

If you've had two or more kids, I'm guessing you'd agree the second time is different. It was for me. I found I could use the experience with my first to help inform how to care for my second, but this didn't mean I knew what I was doing with my second baby. I knew a bit more about what to do, but it was still a learning process.

Chapter 12.

# Brain changes forever[144]

Will the effects of motherhood on the brain last forever? And, more importantly, will your mom brain ever be like it was before? These are great questions. My short answer would be—once a parent always a parent—but that doesn't mean your brain will be the same today as it will be in 5, 10 or even 40 years. It is ever changing in relation to the needs of your child, your biology and what is going on around you.

## Aging gracefully

In 2019, a leading journal of scientific research (*Proceedings of the National Academy of Sciences*), published the first paper[145] using neuroimaging data to investigate how motherhood may affect the brain in 50-60 year old women, many years after they became mothers. Prior to this work, the human data only showed an effect of motherhood on the brain up to two years postpartum[146], but research in animal models had suggested more enduring effects of motherhood on the brain[147].

The study, headed by Dr. Ann-Marie de Lange, the director of the Femilab at the University of Lausanne, and a recent guest on *Mommy Brain Revisited*[148], looked at the relationship between the number of children birthed and markers of brain aging in 12,021 brain images of middle-aged women (50-60 years old) provided from the UK Biobank.[149]

(Note—with that number of participants this data is very robust). Ann-Marie and her team investigated structural brain characteristics in grey matter from brain images (via MRI) and used machine learning to derive biomarkers of global brain aging. They aimed to determine if measures of brain age differed between mothers and non-mothers, as well as the impact of number of births on these brain measures.

What did this brain imaging data show? Women who had given birth had younger-looking brains in middle-age and this effect was related to the number of children they had. Having up to four children may be optimal for this younger-looking brain effect. Interesting! Not only is having children decreasing the age of your brain, the number of children you have may be important too. It should be noted that factors such as age at menarche, age at menopause and number of incomplete pregnancies were controlled for as these factors can also affect the brain.

## Your brain is younger, but how much younger?

First of all, you should know that the age of the brain was estimated using complex algorithms based on its structural characteristics observed by MRI. Having a "younger" brain means that, for your age, the structural characteristics of your brain, based on normal aging models, appear younger. According to the data presented by Ann-Marie, it seems that the brains of mothers are about six months younger than those of non-mothers. This is not a huge difference, but it is significant.

More recently, research from Ann-Marie's team showed that not only is the brain of women who had children younger in appearance, but also that motherhood has enduring effects on certain brain regions[150]. This time, the researchers examined brain images from 19,787 middle- and older-aged women (age range from 45-82 years). They confirmed their previous findings, but they also found that certain brain areas were particularly younger. These brain areas included the amygdala, hippocampus, thalamus, accumbens and putamen—areas important for aspects of maternal caregiving and that play a role in the parental caregiving network, which I previously talked about.

The study further notes that the accumbens was most notably affected. The accumbens is part of the motivation and reward processing system in the brain: we know it plays an important role in wanting to care for baby in the early postpartum period. How and why the accumbens continues to be affected by childbirth decades later is intriguing but, perhaps, speaks the on-going motivation to care for your child. My mom regularly talks with me and my siblings (we are four). In fact, I talk to her nearly every day. She also loves to see me, her youngest, even 40 years later. I'm still "rewarding" for her.

## Grey versus white?

Recently, Ann-Marie's team has taken things one step further and looked at white matter in the aging brain in relation to childbirth[151]. White matter is a type of tissue in the central nervous system that is easy to see in the brain because it is indeed paler than the rest of the brain (called grey matter). It is made up of myelinated axons, i.e. nerve fibres, which are grouped together in bundles allowing the different regions of the brain to communicate with each other. To simplify things, an increase in the amount of white matter would be an indicator of improved communication between different parts of the brain. As in their previous studies, the researchers used thousands of brain images from the UK Biobank. To be exact, they used brain images of 8,895 women aged 54-81 years. The researchers found, similar to previous work looking at grey matter, that more childbirths were related to younger-looking global levels of white matter, which potentially indicates "a protective effect of parity on white matter later in life". They also found a decrease in brain age in several white matter tracts in the brain, most notably the corpus callosum, a tract that connects the left and right cerebral hemispheres, enabling communication between them. The authors don't speculate on how these changes in white matter may affect brain function overall, but I suspect increased white matter would be related to increased communication within and between brain structures. But, then again, this may be a false assumption. Future studies are needed.

It should also be noted that you don't have to have children to have an optimally functioning brain. During our conversation on *Mommy Brain Revisited*, Ann-Marie explained that "it's important to stress that these effects are quite moderate or small. So, whether you have children or not will definitely not determine how healthy your brain is when you age... there are so many factors that influence how we age." This is important to note.

Perhaps what's even more important is that we need to start to consider the impact that reproduction has on a woman's brain later in life, and investigate, in more detail, what role motherhood has on aging processes such as menopause, as well as age-related diseases such as Alzheimer's disease.

## Becoming a parent, the fountain of youth for the brain?

Your mom brain is looking younger as you age, but how is this related to function? And what about dads?

In 2020, a study by researchers at the University of California[152] also looked at brain aging, but investigated it in both middle-aged mothers and fathers. Similar to the studies of Ann-Marie, mentioned above, they used a large sample of brain images from the UK Biobank, including both mothers and fathers. They analyzed biological parameters associated with brain aging, and studied how these measures may be related to visual memory in middle-aged parents. They found that younger-looking brains were evident in mothers and fathers that had 2-3 children, in comparison to people of the same age who didn't have children. They also found that having a child was associated with better visual memory and faster response times during the memory task (as I mentioned in Chapter 5).

These results suggest that younger-looking brains could be linked to improved memory later in life, but also that it's not just the physiology of pregnancy and childbirth that is important—a number of lifestyle factors, including experience in parenting, are likely key contributors to these younger-looking brains in both mothers and fathers.

The research led by Dr. Winnie Orchard[153] (also referred to in Chapter 5) showed that mothers in their 70s had better verbal memory than non-mothers at the same age, and suggests that this improved memory could be linked to changes in cortical thickness in aging mothers. Using brain imaging techniques in 45 aged women and 35 aged men (in their 70s) she found that grey matter thickness varied in parents, and these effects were brain region specific. In mothers in their 70s, (compared to non-mothers in their 70s) they found increased cortical thickness in the parahippocampal gyrus, a brain region involved in memory formation (where increased cortical thickness has been associated with better memory in old age). Another brain region that was affected in aged mothers was the dorsolateral prefrontal cortex, a brain area important for mothering early in the postpartum period.

In fathers who were in their 70s, one of the most notable changes was a decrease in cortical thickness of the anterior cingulate cortex, a brain area involved in social cognition and affected by parenting in the early postpartum period in fathers. This data shows that both mothers and fathers have effects of parenting on their brains into late life, but that these effects are different, likely due to differences in involvement with their children or additional factors that have yet to be explored.

Recent work from Winnie and her co-authors goes beyond these structural brain changes to look at functional changes in aging parents. Again, they looked at brain function in 70-year-old[154] parents but this time using fMRI activity—focusing on blood flow. They found that in mothers (those that either birthed or perhaps adopted—they didn't have the data on this), but not in fathers, there was "widespread decreasing functional connectivity with increasing number of children parented". This means that decades after having become a mother, the activity of the maternal brain undergoes many changes which contribute to a brain that is "younger".

Parenthood has lasting structural and functional effects on the brain, but how? Recent literature suggests that hormonal and immunological factors are involved—at least this is a theory that needs to be tested experimentally. However, it should not be forgotten that in addition to these biological factors, and as Dr. Winnie Orchard said on my podcast[155], "parenthood is a continuum of experience, and can represent a learning environment that is sustained over decades of an individual's life." A learning environment that has the potential to change the brain of every parent.

# Part 3
# Parents are made, not born

Chapter 13.

# Birth doesn't make a mother

I grew up on a small farm where we raised many different animals. I loved my rabbits, minilops to be precise; my mom loved her bantam hens and every spring there were a number of little chicks running around; and my brother, Rhett, had all kinds of ducks and other birds (we even had peacocks for a time). Among this menagerie of birds were some rather strange ducks, called Indian Runner Ducks, which almost seemed to stand straight up and walk around like humans. The females weren't very good at sitting on their eggs to hatch them, so we placed some eggs from the ducks under a broody bantam hen of my mom's. This little black hen seemed happy as could be to have these rather large eggs under her. After a few weeks, adorable yellow ducklings hatched and the mother hen was proud to parade her "chicks" around the barnyard and try to teach them how to become chickens.

Eventually the four little yellow ducklings grew into rather large white ducks that towered over the little black hen, but they still followed her around the yard. After all, she was their mother. One day, the ducklings discovered the water pool we had put out for the other ducks and jumped right in the water. Their mother, the bantam hen, was not happy—what chick is supposed to do that?!—and after much clucking and severe scolding from their mom, the ducklings left the water pool and followed her back to the yard. They listened and obeyed, as my mother would say.

This was perhaps my first experience with adoption. More specifi-cally cross-species adoption, which is not something we see very often in the animal kingdom, but it definitely exists. (Did you ever see that cat that adopted ducklings on that farm in Ireland?[156])

## All mothers

A number of types of mothers exist. And I believe that none are born, all are made—regardless of whether they are a birthing mother or not. It takes time and experience to figure out how to parent. That is reality. Of course, birthing mothers may have a slight advantage as they've had a few extra months of experiencing a baby (during pregnancy); they also experience many hormonal changes during pregnancy, birth and post-partum that prepare them to learn quickly how to become parents. But, of course, anyone can become a parent, and becoming a mother is not defined solely by giving birth.

Among the "non-biological" mothers are stepmothers, foster moth-ers, and adoptive mothers (and here I'm including same-sex parents as well). I read recently that, in 2019, in France, more than 216,000 women are stepmothers[157], due to the increase in blended families. These mater-nal roles are, of course, accompanied by different degrees of experience, involvement and responsibility. For example, an adoptive mother may have her child from shortly after birth or when the child is a little older; a stepmother may have her stepchildren every day or only one day every other week; a foster mother may have foster children for weeks, months or years. Regardless, these mothers are mothers and are often indistin-guishable from birth mothers after the initial days or weeks of parenting.

## Enriched brain

Although much of the research that I've talked about in this book has been on neurobiological changes in biological mothers, there is research starting to look at neurobiological changes in non-biological mothers—that is to say, in those who become mothers without being related to the child by blood. We need much more research on the neurobiology of all mothers and parents because, as it is now, we know very little about non-birthing mothers—from a neurobiological but also a biological standpoint.

Years ago, now, when I was doing my doctoral research, I looked at the brains and behavior of adoptive mother rats. At the time, I wasn't interested in the idea of how adoption affects the brain per se. I was focused on whether pregnancy, birth and experience with offspring were all needed for the brain changes that we see in mothers, or whether it was only experience with offspring, or just pregnancy that were necessary. I didn't have the time and resources to completely answer these questions but what I did show[158] was that there are brain changes with adoption in female rats that are different than what I saw in birthing mothers.

I should also mention that female rats don't readily adopt offspring, especially if they haven't mothered before. However, by repeatedly giving them exposure to offspring (who were fed by lactating females), these non-experienced rats become "mothers" and show mother-typical behaviors toward the offspring, such as licking and grooming them, retrieving them to the nest and hovering over them to keep them warm.

What I found in my research with these adoptive mother rats was that they showed different changes in new neuron production in the hippocampus (a brain area I spend most of my time studying due to its role in memory and mental health) than biological mother rats. More specifically adoptive mother rats showed an increase in neurogenesis in the hippocampus with offspring exposure, while birthing mother rats showed a decrease in hippocampal neurogenesis[159].

We're not sure why there were these differences between adoptive and birthing mother rats, but one thing that seems to be playing a role is the enriching experience of the offspring on the adoptive maternal brain. A large body of research has shown that having enriched environments[160] can increase hippocampal neurogenesis, thus this is likely a case in these adoptive mother rats. It is also likely that the different physiology, or the lack of the changes in pregnancy and lactational hormones, play a role. Regardless, the adoptive mother rats mothered effectively, showing typical maternal behaviors, suggesting to me that there are some similar brain changes between non-birthing and birthing mothers. We need to do more research in different areas of the brain to understand them...

# Impact without birth

When talking about human mothers, there exists, as far as I know, only two or three studies looking at non-birthing mothers and how their brain changes with motherhood. In the first[161], headed by Prof. Johanna Bick at the University of Houston, Texas, the primary focus of the study was to see if oxytocin, a peptide hormone associated with the mother-infant bond in birthing mothers, was also related to the mother-infant bond in non-biological mothers. The study was also designed to look at whether oxytocin levels in a foster mother were associated with their brain activity in response to viewing a picture of their foster child, using electrophysiological measurements called event-related potentials (ERP), and how "delighted" they were with their foster children (measured through behavioral observations[162]). Overall, 41 foster mother-infant pairs participated in the study. The infants were on average 8.5 months of age (ranging in age from 2 weeks to 35 months of age at the start of the study). The results showed that, as with birthing mothers, foster mothers' oxytocin levels were associated with their feelings of delight toward their foster infant and how their brain responded to a picture of an infant. What is also interesting is that, over time, or with a longer period of fostering the infant, the level of oxytocin in the foster mother in response to cuddling the infant became linked specifically to her brain response to the image of her foster infant (and not when she saw another infant). Thus, with experience mothering, the brain and hormone changes in the foster mother are adapted to the foster child. Again, experience matters.

In another study[163], led by Dr. Marisela Hernández-González and her colleagues, the researchers measured specific types of brain activity with electroencephalogram (EEG) in groups of biological mothers, adoptive mothers and non-mothers in response to viewing a video of a 4-month-old baby girl smiling, crying or with a neutral expression. Each group consisted of ten women. The study found that biological and adoptive mothers had the same EEG response to the smiling baby video, which likely indicated pleasure in response to the smiling baby. Interestingly, when looking at the crying baby video, adoptive mothers had elevated EEG activity compared to biological mothers, indicating that adoptive mothers had a brain that was more reactive to the upset baby. The non-mothers, not surprisingly, were different than the mothers in brain activation, showing a general activation of the brain that could be interpreted as meaning that they found all baby-related videos unpleasant or uninteresting. This suggests that the experience of mothering is important to the changes in the brain seen in this (and other) studies.

These same researchers[164] also studied cortical synchronization, that is to say the way the prefrontal cortex and temporal cortex were activated at the same time, in biological and adoptive mothers, while listening to a baby cry. They found that biological mothers, but not adoptive mothers, had reduced synchronization between the prefrontal cortex and temporal cortex. Because the prefrontal cortex is partly involved in inhibition in the temporal cortex, this reduction in synchronization, and so the absence of inhibition, may indicate an emotional involvement more profound and acute in response to a baby cry. However, this could also mean that adoptive mothers perceived the baby cries as less unpleasant. Regardless, all mothers in this study had similar results to the mother attachment tests and reported feeling "alarmed" whenever a baby cried. It seems that their brain just reacted differently.

Of course, there are a number of questions that need to be answered to fully understand how the brains of non-birthing and non-biological mothers change when they are made mothers, but what we are seeing, and I suspect we will see more of, is that experience and positive mother -infant bonds are important to facilitate the biological correlates of motherhood in non-birthing mothers.

## Simply a mother

On November 30th, 2021, Josephine Baker, perhaps the most famous adoptive mother in France during the last century, was inducted into France's Pantheon. She was "A world-renowned artist, a member of the Resistance and tireless anti-racist activist... involved in all the battles that unite righteous and willing citizens in France and across the world" said Macron, the French President. She was an extraordinary person. Josephine was also the mother of the "Rainbow Tribe" (she had adopted twelve kids of diverse nationalities) and brought much needed attention to the value of adoption. One of her sons said this about her; "She was our mother... We don't count ourselves as adopted, we are the sons and daughters of Josephine Baker." She was a mother. Not an adoptive mother, but just simply a mother and I bet her brain reflected that too.

Chapter 14.

# Daddy brain

L et's talk about dads for a minute or two. To be honest, I don't think a lot about how a dad's brain changes with parenting, but there is a growing body of research on this subject. While not exhaustive, I am going to address some key points.

## Changing role

Traditionally, it was fathers who worked outside of the home. They were the authoritarians, the heads of the household, and not the parent involved in everyday child-rearing. When I was little, my dad filled part of this traditional role. He was often away working on construction sites throughout my home province of British Columbia, Canada. When he was home (usually for longer spells in the winter, if I remember correctly), we had a lot of fun: we went snowmobiling on the lake when it was frozen, we went to Disneyland for Christmas (we went three times by car—that's 24h of driving!), I worked with him in the garage on cold winter evenings, and so on.

As I've grown up and had my own children, I've seen that the role of a father has changed considerably. Today, fathers are spending more and more time with their children, even research supports this[165]. But often, many socio-cultural and individual differences result in a wide range of how a father is involved in childrearing; from complete absence to that of the primary caregiver[166].

I think this wide range in the role of a father or partner is still very much socially dependent. Looking back on our own experience as parents, I remember instances where my husband's role as an "involved" father wasn't easy. One story in particular comes to mind. When our youngest was still in diapers we spent the day at the Keukenhof, one of the world's largest flower gardens, in Holland, enjoying the beautiful spring flowers. Our little one needed a diaper change, and as usual, my husband planned to take him to the public bathroom to do so. Off he went only to return seconds later to report in frustration there was no baby change table in the men's bathroom. How? Why? I suggested going straight into the women's bathroom where I'd earlier seen a change table. And he did. Sometimes you have to do what you have to do. I might add that the women in the bathroom were quite impressed with it all and didn't mind a bit.

## Does size matter?[167]

Studying the paternal brain is a great way to study how experience parenting shapes the brain. As with studies in mothers, both brain structure and function have been investigated in human fathers, but not always to the same extent or in the same way. Let's look at structural brain changes we know of so far.

Research by Dr. Elseline Hoekzema, that I already mentioned (refer to Chapter 9), showed significant reductions in grey matter volume of a number of brain areas in mothers across pregnancy but these same changes were not evident in fathers, or at least aren't quite the same. Of the few additional neuroimaging studies looking at the changes in grey matter volume in fathers' brains, research is showing that there are some structural brain changes that likely depend on when, during the perinatal period, the study takes place. In one study[168] by Kim and colleagues where changes in grey matter volume were investigated in 16 biological dads between 2-4 weeks postpartum and 12-16 weeks postpartum, the results showed that during this early postpartum time period fathers had increased volumes of brain regions associated with reward and attachment, such as the hypothalamus, amygdala, and the striatum, and with mentalization (e.g. PFC, subgenual cingulate and superior temporal gyrus). These brain volume increases were similar to what the same group of researchers reported in biological mothers at similar timepoints[169].

The researchers also found reductions in grey matter volumes in the dad's brain in regions involved in processing threat and parenting stress (e.g. orbitofrontal cortex), salience (e.g. insula), and also mentalization (e.g. posterior cingulate cortex, precuneus and MPFC). In addition, they found an association between the decreases in volume of the orbitofrontal cortex in fathers and increased intrusive parenting behaviors[170].

More recently, a neuroimaging study lead by Dr. Susana Carmona and colleagues[171] looked at cortical volume, thickness and surface area of a number of brain areas important for parenting in 20 first-time fathers, before their partner's pregnancy and at two months postpartum, in comparison to brain changes in a group of 17 childless men. (This study used the same participants as Hoekzema et al. one, 2017[172], but analyzed the brain images of fathers in a different way.) This study found reductions in volume and thickness from preconception-to-postpartum in a brain area called the precuneus. The more the reductions in the volume and thickness of this brain area, the greater the father's neural response to pictures of his baby. These reductions were less pronounced and affected fewer regions, compared to those observed in the mothers.

What does this mean? Size does seem to matter, and it's likely that pregnancy-related cues or the anticipation of the baby may be primers for brain changes in fathers. We know that hormone levels in fathers change during pregnancy and postpartum. For example, there are increases in oxytocin and prolactin and decreases in testosterone[173]. These hormones could be key players in the brain changes in fathers[174] during pregnancy and beyond. Of course, interacting with the infant during the early postpartum weeks is also a key factor shaping grey matter volume changes in the paternal brain, but who is to say whether interacting with the fetus during pregnancy (i.e., feeling it move) doesn't have effects on a dad's brain as well?

## When a dad's brain becomes pregnant

In line with this idea of pregnancy changing the dad's brain in a structural way, a recent study[175] looked at how a man's brain activity may change when his partner is early in her first pregnancy (20 weeks gestation). This study compared brain functional changes (fMRI) in 36 childless men and 36 first-time expectant fathers while viewing a video of a person interacting with an infant (playing or changing a diaper) or a non-infant-related video. One of the most interesting findings from this study is that there was an association between the partner's gestational age and the expectant father's activation of two parenting-related brain areas, the left inferior frontal gyrus and the amygdala, in response to videos of interacting with an infant. These results imply that, at least with regards to some brain areas, a father's brain starts to develop during early pregnancy.

Apart from this study, most of the neuroimaging studies on the paternal brain have looked at how a father's brain in the postpartum period responds to photos, videos or cries of infants. There are some interesting studies out there and here are a couple of my favorites.

## Responding to baby

A recent study, by Prof. James (Jim) Rilling and colleagues[176] at Emory University, investigated how a father's behavior toward his infant affected the activity of his brain. In this study, brain responses in 20 new fathers were measured by fMRI, four months after birth, while passively listening to an infant cry (not a fun thing to do) or actively attempting to console the crying infant by selecting soothing strategies in a video game format. The study found that when, compared to passively listening to an infant cry, actively responding to the baby activated brain regions involved in movement, empathy and motivation, while deactivating brain regions involved in stress and anxiety. Fathers that reported more frustration with the task, had less activation in brain areas involved in emotional regulation, such as the prefrontal cortex and the supplementary motor area. Fathers who successfully soothed an infant in the video game showed greater neural activation in areas involved in action-outcome learning, mentalization, and salience processing (e.g. anterior cingulate cortex and posterior cingulate cortex). This study is exciting in that it provides further evidence of brain areas underlying parenting. It also shows quite simply that how we respond to an infant affects our brain.

## Mom versus Dad

There are not many studies specifically comparing brain activation to an infant in both mothers and fathers. One study[177]—that I love—investigates brain activity in primary caregiver mothers and fathers, and compares it to secondary caregiver fathers. This is a great way to investigate how gender and parental investment affect the parental brain. That is—how does the brain of a primary caregiver biological mom and a primary caregiver dad (in this case a dad who had a child through surrogacy with his partner) compare, and how may they differ from a secondary caregiver biological dad?

In total, 89 parents participated in this study carried out by Prof. Eyal Abraham and their colleagues. Brain imaging was done while the parents watched videos of themselves playing with their one-year-old infant and a video of a stranger playing with another infant of a similar age. Results of this study are compelling and speak to the role of experience. More specifically, the researchers found that compared to secondary caregiver fathers, primary caregiver mothers and primary caregiver fathers showed greater activation in the amygdala, a central hub of the ancient parental brain circuit. The two groups of fathers showed greater activation in the superior temporal sulcus (which plays a role in social perception, among other things) compared to mothers. It's interesting to note here, that the more time a father reported spending with his child, the higher the functional connectivity between these two brain areas. These findings show that there is overlap in brain activity between mothers and fathers that depends on time spent with the child. However, there are also differences. Experience matters but so do sex/gender and likely the experience of pregnancy.

## What about testosterone?

I recently spoke with Prof. Jim Rilling on my podcast *Mommy Brain Revisited*[178] about brain changes in human fathers. He's done a number of interesting studies on this subject and the role of oxytocin and testosterone in these changes. One of his studies[179], that is perhaps one of his most well-known, compares brain activity in fathers and non-fathers while they look at photos of babies or photos of sexually motivating stimuli (in other words, porn). Amusing, right? One reason he did this study was because there is an idea that hormone changes affect empathic responding to children, which is important for parenting and child development. Another reason is that the hormone changes in new fathers may be part of the trade-off between mating and parenting effort—new fathers may focus more on parenting and not mating. To test these ideas, the study compared brain activity (fMRI) of 88 heterosexual biological fathers of children between 1-2 years of age and 50 heterosexual non-fathers that were unmarried and at least 25 years of age, while looking at photos of an unknown child or women in "sexually provocative clothing and poses", as well as various control photos. Blood samples were taken to investigate oxytocin and testosterone levels.

When looking at pictures of a child, fathers showed stronger brain activation than non-fathers in brain regions important for face emotion processing (caudal middle frontal gyrus), mentalizing (temporo-parietal junction) and reward processing (medial orbitofrontal cortex). Non-fathers had significantly stronger neural responses to sexually provocative images in regions important for reward and approach-related motivation (dorsal caudate and nucleus accumbens). Not surprisingly, fathers had higher oxytocin and lower testosterone levels than non-fathers. Interestingly, higher levels of activity in the caudal middle frontal gyrus when viewing a photo of a child was associated with a lower level of testosterone in fathers. Surprisingly, neither testosterone nor oxytocin levels predicted neural responses to sexual stimuli.

From this work and that of others, it looks like the decline in testosterone with fatherhood is a good thing and helps a father's brain respond to his child's needs. I'm not sure how well this idea of lower testosterone with fatherhood is accepted by fathers, or men in general, but it's not all about testosterone. Other studies[180] have examined how brain activity in mothers and fathers, in response to infant cues, is associated with other hormones and the levels of neuropeptides (very small proteins, for example oxytocin). A study by Dr. Atzil and their colleagues showed that when parents watched a video of their child, mothers showed higher activation of the amygdala, and the response of the amygdala in mothers was associated with the levels of oxytocin in the blood. Fathers also showed activation in the amygdala, but this activation was correlated with levels of vasopressin, another hormone, and not oxytocin. This research also showed that the brains of mothers and fathers respond in a similar way to their infant in brain regions such as the anterior cingulate cortex, the motor and premotor cortex, the cerebellum, the medial and lateral prefrontal cortex, the temporal cortex and the insula. This suggests that mothers and fathers coordinate their brain responses to infant cues. This proposed brain synchrony between parents would be fascinating to explore further.

## Everything that you need

I want to point out that there is a growing body of research in certain biparental animal species showing the complexity of brain changes with fatherhood. One recent study showed that in both male and female mice there are neurons in the hypothalamus, neurons expressing galanine[181], that are essential for parenting. This is the work from Prof. Catherine Dulac and her colleagues at Harvard University. I spoke with Catherine about her research[182] and this is what she said about fathers: "Dads have an essential role to play in parenting and they have all it takes in their brains for that role". I think we need to remember that.

Chapter 15.

# Grandma brain

I often think of my Grandma, my dad's mom. I grew up in the same town as my paternal grandparents and spent many Sunday dinners at their place, celebrated Ukrainian holidays (the parents of my grandmother were from Ukraine), and learned how to braid, weave, sew and cross stitch (and many other things) from my Grandma. We also made a lot of *perogies* with her (yum!). With my grandfather I watched a lot of hockey (according to my Grandpa the Edmonton Oilers were the best, particularly when Gretzky (#99) was at the top of his game).

My mom, on the other hand, did not have a Ukrainian heritage but had a German and Scottish (and possibly Irish horse-thief) heritage. As long as we had shortbread and periodically listened to bagpipes, in addition to our Ukrainian traditions, she was happy. My mom's mom, my Nana, liked children to be seen and not heard. Dinners at her place were less frequent. When we did go to visit her, my brother and I spent the afternoon in the woods with my older sister being petrified that a cougar was going to eat us... (and yes, there were cougars in the region, not to mention the fact that Nana had a cougar rug in her living room).

My paternal Grandma played a significant role in my life. Not only for the aspects related to my heritage and culture as a Canadian, but also in terms of her role as a woman. My late aunt, her daughter, told me that my Grandma "was a bra burner before her time". Indeed, she was. She was a strong woman, who stood her ground and made her way, even in a traditional role as a farmer's daughter and a farmer's wife. I could share so many stories about how she and my Grandpa impacted my life but, I'm here to talk about the brain so let's get to it...

## Grand-mommy brain?

In 2017, when I was co-organizing the 6th Parental Brain meeting in Toronto, Canada, which brings together international experts who study the parental brain, I remember thinking how amazing it would be to have some work on how grandparenting affects the brain. Are grandparents' brains activated by their grandchildren in the same way as they are with their children? Are grandma's brains different than grandpa's brains? If there are brain changes in grandparents, do they relate to how much a grandparent cares for their children? Does it matter if they are maternal or paternal grandparents? Does having grandchildren impact brain health in grandparents? Oh, so many questions and oh, so few answers. In fact, at the time I couldn't find a single article published on the topic. Not one.

Fast forward to the fall of 2021, when I heard that Prof. Jim Rilling (The same Jim Rilling mentioned in the previous chapter) was doing some research on grandparenting and the brain. As you can imagine, I was very excited. I spoke with Jim primarily about his work on fatherhood and the brain, which I discussed in the previous chapter, and he sent me a copy of his manuscript on brain changes in grandmothers prior to publication. It was later published [183] and received quite a bit of publicity.

This study was partially based on the *Grandmother Hypothesis* from evolutionary anthropology which, in Jim's words, posits that "a human female's post-menopausal longevity evolved because of the benefits grandmothers were able to bestow on their grandchildren". In other words, animals are generally programmed to live until they reach sexual maturity (and then to die out once they are no longer fertile). In humans, grandmothers started living longer because they could help to raise their grandchildren. This hypothesis was established by different scientific observations which show that the presence of a maternal grandmother is beneficial for child survival, at least up to a point. According to Jim, the research shows that "Grandmothers can also increase their daughter's fertility, and hence their own inclusive fitness, by decreasing their daughter's interbirth interval". How cool is that?

To me, it makes sense that an extra pair of hands would be beneficial when you have children; someone to help with childcare or food preparation, laundry, housecleaning, errands etc. How this Grandmother Hypothesis works biologically isn't clear, but we now know that changes in the brain of grandmas are important.

In their research, Jim and his colleagues recruited 50 grandmothers who had at least one biological grandchild between 3 and 12 years of age. They used fMRI brain imaging techniques to see how a grandmother's brain was activated in response to a photo of her grandchild. They also investigated the way the brain of the grandmothers responded to a photo of an unknown child of the same sex, race and age as her grandchild (to have a control comparison), the parent of the grandchild that was the same sex as the grandchild and an unknown adult of the same sex, race and age as the parent. Grandmas were also asked how involved they were with their grandchild and how attached they felt toward them.

What did they find? First of all, grandmothers showed brain activation in main regions of the parental brain when viewing their grandchild, compared to viewing an unknown child of the same age and sex. These main brain areas (medial preoptic area, midbrain—substantia nigra and ventral tegmental area, nucleus accumbens, caudate nucleus, anterior cingulate cortex, dorsomedial prefrontal cortex, for example) are important for aspects of parental behavior, motivation, emotional empathy and theory of mind, as in parents. This suggests that the parental brain neurocircuitry is activated when caring for a child, whether you are the parent or grandparent.

## Nothing like Grandma's love

It is interesting to note that many parental brain regions were more activated when a grandmother looked at a photo of her child (or the partner of her child) than when she looked at a photo of her grandchild, with the exception of brain regions important for emotional empathy (the insula and the somatosensory cortex). Grandmothers showed more activation in brain areas important for emotional empathy when viewing their grandchild compared to viewing their child or spouse of their child or another child. The amount of involvement or how attached a grandmother felt toward her grandchild wasn't highly correlated with these measures of brain activation. This suggests that just being a grandmother and having a basic level of engagement with a grandchild is enough to activate the grandmaternal brain. Definitely future research is needed to better understand how these brain changes in grandmothers are related to her interactions with her grandchild.

What I do find striking from this research is:

- the parental brain regions are activated in grandmothers in response to their grandchild AND their child;

- Grandmothers show greater activation in brain areas important for emotional empathy when looking at pictures of their grandchild than when looking at pictures of the grandchild's parent (their child).

These findings are important and beg that question of whether grandmothers may be more connected to grandchildren than to their own offspring, as an article from *The Guardian*[184] points out. Maybe, but maybe their relationship with their grandchild is simply different.

## It takes a village to raise a child

When I spoke with Jim about this study, I still had so many questions. What about grandfathers, maternal versus paternal grandparents, the number of grandchildren? He assured me these are all great questions and ones that need to be answered. We joked that perhaps a family neuroscience field needs to be developed to explore the neural connectivity of the social relationships that make up a family tree. Who knows what the future will hold?

As I told a CNN reporter covering this research[185], the bottom line for me is that "this work points to the fact that there are important brain changes in members of a 'village' that raise a child. It's not just the brain of birthing parents and partners that changes."

## Not just grandmas…

I also want to point out that grandfathers are very important too. We don't have the brain research on them presently, but I often see grandfathers involved with their grandchildren. Maybe they are involved in a different way, but that's still beneficial. My Grandpa did different things with us than my Grandma did. With him we watched hockey, as I mentioned, but from him I also learned how to be creative in a different way than with my grandma. He was always inventing things, he was an avid gardener, and he did a lot of odd jobs around our small farm that made things run more smoothly. He also respected my grandma. That was important to see.

Some months ago, I was in Athens working on a project with my friend and collaborator Prof. Christina Dalla at the National and Kapodistrian University of Athens. We talked about the importance of grandparents in Greek society and she told me that they have a saying in Greek that "the child of my child is twice my child". I think there is something to this and maybe that is what is happening in the grandparental brain.

## All parents

Before concluding this section on how the brain changes when we are parents, I want to point out that "parents" and "families" come in many different forms. Parent(s) can consist of a mom and dad, a mom and mom, a dad and dad, a mom, a dad, an aunt and uncle, a grandma, grandparents or a parent by whatever name suits you, who is biological or not. I suspect a fundamental parental brain will exist in all parents, but will be nuanced based on experience—time parenting[186], child temperament, life stress[187], sociocultural factors[188], number of children, and so on—as well as underlying biology. The parental brain is driven to take care of the needs of the child and will adapt accordingly. The adaption and change, that's natural. Parenting is a process of mismatch and reparation. It is about making mistakes and learning from them. It is not instinctual, it develops over time.

# Part 4
# When all is not well in the land of *Bliss*

Chapter 16.

# A short history of maternal madness[189]

The joy of motherhood. The *bliss*. It's something we're all force-fed. "You'll be so happy! It's amazing!" But in reality, motherhood is not always a time of joy and, for some, the "bliss" is never there. I use the term "bliss" because you have probably heard of *Bliss Stories*, the French podcast (and book) on motherhood by Clementine Galey. "*Bliss* is beauty, that moment of grace that happens when you bring a child into the world... this suspended moment", explains Clementine Galey in an interview[190]. What I love about her podcast is the fact that women share their "bliss" stories. All parts of them. The good and the bad. They speak the truth about pregnancy and birth. It's real life. Because motherhood is messy—physically, behaviorally, emotionally. And you know what? It's always been this way.

Motherhood isn't easy, and it is a time when there is an increased risk of mental and physical health problems. In the following chapters, I will focus on mental health struggles—related to depression, anxiety, trauma, psychosis and loss—as research is starting to show they are related to changes in the maternal brain.

First, let's remember that over 75% of women are content, and even happy most of the time, with becoming a mom. But many women struggle with moderate to severe mental illness that is often overlooked or disregarded. These illnesses always have a biological component and likely a neurobiological one.

In fact, the link between perinatal (or maternal) mental illness and the brain isn't a new thing. Mothers have struggled throughout the ages with their mental health. This news may bring you comfort in knowing that you are not alone. The problem is that perinatal mental illness hasn't received the recognition and understanding that it should have, while advancements in other areas of mental health have been made. Fortunately, we are starting to recognize what historical texts talked about—that perinatal mental illness is related to physiological changes of childbirth and these changes are often linked to the maternal brain.[191]

## His story of her story

The first written record of postpartum mental illness is attributed to Hippocrates in 400 B.C.[192]. In his book titled *Epidemics*, he provides brief descriptions of 8-9 cases of postpartum delirium or mania. In these early records new mothers that suffered from delirium or mania appeared to do so as a consequence of a severe infection and fever. This is something we now call *puerperal fever* (from *puer*, child in latin), because it is due to an infection. Today, it is not considered a typical postpartum mental illness.

Nonetheless, there are three things that I find striking about Hippocrates' early descriptions of postpartum delirium. First, he acknowledged a link between birth and mental illness over 2500 years ago. Thank you! Today we know that the immediate postpartum period is a time in a woman's life, particularly a first-time mother, when she is at the greatest risk of being hospitalized for a mental illness[193].

Second, Hippocrates' writings show a link between what we know now as immune function, as evidenced by fever in the women he described, and delirium. Today, we are starting to understand how the immune system may be linked to postpartum mental illness, in the absence of infection and fever, as well as how immune cells in the brain, called microglia, are related to maternal mental health[194].

Third, Hippocrates proposed that the brain is a key source of mental illness postpartum. Hippocrates predicted that lochial discharge—the fluid that comes from the uterus after birth—could flow to the head and result in agitation, delirium and attacks of mania. With our advances in neuroscience we know this exact scenario doesn't exist, but brain changes are definitely involved in all perinatal mental illness, during the postpartum *and* during pregnancy.

But I'm getting ahead of myself, let's continue on the history of peri-natal mental illness. After Hippocrates, the next known reference to a perinatal mental illness was by Trotula of Salerno[195], an 11th century professor of medicine or a 13th century midwife (historical sources don't agree on this point). They wrote: "If the womb is too moist, the brain is filled with water, and the moisture running over the eyes, compels them to involuntarily shed tears." This is a rather beautiful description of postpartum depression. The brain is full of water that it must release and this is done through crying. Like Hippocrates, Trotula attributed post-partum mental illness to fluid buildup in the brain, noting, again, the importance of the connection between bodily fluids and the brain in mental illness after birth.

In the Middle Ages, the idea of perinatal mental illness began to change in Europe. It appears that mental illnesses, not attributed to fever or infection in the new mother, were talked about. These perinatal mental illnesses were referred to as disturbances of the "maternal in-stinct" in new mothers, and ranged from melancholia or feelings of deep sadness, hatred of the newborn and, in extreme cases, infant abuse and infanticide. At this time, society did not have an understanding of these disturbances of "maternal instinct", and often, mothers who exhibited such disturbances were said to be witches or had dabbled in witchcraft. This is not a surprise as many stigmatized individuals of that period, often women, were considered witches. They were burned at the stake or subject to whatever punishment was the current fashion.

When I was 12 years old, I went to Edinburgh, Scotland with my mom. During a tour, I remember being told that during the Middle Ages if a woman was considered a witch she was thrown into the river. If she survived there was no doubt that she was a witch and she would then be burned at the stake. If she drowned in the river this meant that she was not a witch. This was obviously a lose-lose situation. Thankfully, today, we don't physically burn mothers at the stake if they have a mental illness, but too often we stigmatize them as "bad mothers"—so perhaps we haven't changed that much?

Until the 1800s, disturbances of maternal instinct often referred to postpartum melancholia and delirium. However, anxiety and obsessions in new mothers were also written about as early as the 1600s, but they did not get the attention they deserved.

It wasn't until the mid-1800s that we began to see an acknowledgement of the impact of pregnancy, birth, and postpartum on mental health in birthing people outside of fever-induced delirium. Interestingly, these "maternal conditions" were not always considered mental maladies, especially when it came to psychosis and infanticide, but were considered part of forensic medicine—"an area of medicine dealing with the application of medical knowledge to establish facts in civil or criminal legal cases, such as an investigation into the cause and time of a suspicious death". Take, for example, one of the first non-fever-related postpartum delirium cases written about by Jean-Etienne Esquirol, a Parisian physician, in 1845. Note, that he does not see this case fitting for his book on mental maladies (What?!): "Neither will I speak of the delirium of those who, in their phrens, destroy the children to whom they have just given birth. False shame, perplexity, fear, misery and crime, do not always lead to infanticide. Delirium however, by disturbing the reason of the recently confined, sometimes also, directs their sacrilegious hands. A maiden becomes pregnant, does not conceal the fact, ... and announces the expected event to all. She is confined during the night. On the following day, she is found in her bed and the child in the privy [dead from stabbing]... Has not this young woman suffered from an attack of delirium? Finally, this and other facts of similar import, belong to legal medicine, and ought not to occupy me here[196]."

## Merci Marcé!

It wasn't until 1858 when Louis-Victor Marcé, a French physician, who studied under Esquirol, wrote an entire book on psychiatric disorders of women during and following pregnancy. The book titled *Traité de la folie des femmes enceintes* was the first of its kind and recorded illnesses during the entire transition to motherhood; throughout pregnancy and postpartum. Thank you Marcé! He notes that the most common mental illness during this time is depression (melancholia) and that mania and manic-depressive symptoms can also be evident. He also noted that the symptoms of these mental illnesses decreased as pregnancy progressed, something we're not clear about today.

What I find interesting is that Marcé didn't view pregnancy as a time of joy and fulfillment, especially for those women with pre-existing mental illness. At the time, physicians were "prescribing" pregnancy as a treatment for women who suffered from mental maladies (!); Marcé was very much against this practice, rightfully so. He knew that pregnancy did not always make a woman happy. And, by the way, when did we start to think that pregnancy and motherhood were analogous to happiness?

Marcé recorded that postpartum mental illnesses were the most frequent and severe of all perinatal "insanities"[197]. He wrote about mania, melancholia, delusional states, and other psychotic illnesses and noted that they sometimes showed unusual features postpartum, compared to other times in life. He acknowledged the complexity of these postpartum disorders and the fact that they may not occur during the immediate postpartum but could become evident months later. Although he doesn't remark much on perinatal anxiety, specifically, he does note that: "Where subjects [women] are predisposed to mental illness through either hereditary antecedents, previous illnesses, or through an excessive nervous susceptibility, pregnancy, delivery and lactation can have disastrous repercussions."

Marcé's comprehensive text on perinatal mental illness didn't get the recognition that it deserved when it was published in 1858, but his legacy has lived on. Perhaps his name is most recognized in *The International Marcé Society for Perinatal Mental Health*[198], an "interdisciplinary organization dedicated to supporting research and assistance surrounding prenatal and postpartum mental health for mothers, fathers and their babies". I'd like to think that Marcé would be astonished by what he has inspired.

## After Marcé

In the late 1800s, Emil Kraepelin, a German physician, wrote more about the relationship between childbirth-related psychiatric disorders and, particularly, manic-depressive illness. He writes that *amentia* "... an acute state of dreamlike confusion, illusionary or hallucinatory distortion of reality and motor agitation" often occurs after childbirth. Today, we would likely refer to *amentia* as postpartum psychosis, but Kraepelin also described amentia as being accompanied by depressed mood, thus pointing to a bipolar disorder. Kraepelin stressed that childbirth is a potent trigger for mood episodes in women, but also noted that pregnancy could have a protective effect against depression in some patients with manic-depressive illness. Interestingly, there is research today supporting these first ideas that pregnancy can have positive effects on the course of bipolar disorder in some women[199].

As with Marcé, Kraepelin's work on the role of pregnancy and the postpartum period on perinatal manic-depressive illness was overlooked by many, but his descriptions and ideas hold true today. For example, key points from Kraepelin's work showed that birth, lack of sleep and a history of a mental illness were contributing factors to the onset of postpartum manic-depressive illness. Thanks to current research, these are all factors we know can increase the risk of developing symptoms of bipolar disorder postpartum.

In the mid to late 1900s, a psychiatrist in London, Dr. Channi Kumar[200], was a key figure in the development of perinatal psychiatry as a specialty. He was internationally recognized for his research into the causes, consequences and treatment of postpartum mental illness. One of Kumar's greatest achievements was in raising awareness, in public, medical and academic arenas, about postpartum mental illness and its impact on mothers, their baby and family. He was a founding member of *The International Marcé Society*, mentioned earlier.

## Other heroes and sheroes

As you can see, throughout history a number of men have championed our current understanding of perinatal mental illness. More recently, *heroes* and *sheroes* have come to the forefront from a range of professional backgrounds and with lived experience. Some women leading the way to improving awareness and treatments of perinatal mental illnesses that come to my mind today are largely based in the USA: Dr. Katherine Wisner, Karen Kleiman (Founder of Postpartum Stress), Dr. Samantha Meltzer-Brody, Alanis Morrisette.... In France there are a number of clinicians that should be mentioned including Dr. Nine Glangeaud, Dr. Jacques Dayan and Dr. Michel Dugnat. Globally, we could add many to this list. Fortunately, there are many champions for increasing our awareness and understanding of perinatal mental illness.

Perinatal mental illnesses are very much biological events that are linked to neuroscience, experience and physiology. They are treatable illnesses. As our research and understanding improves, we can add to our growing list of interventions and preventative measures to improve the lives of mothers, and fathers, who suffer in silence. But advances in improving maternal health can only be made when governments, research institutions, health care providers, scientists and the general public see the mental health of parents as a priority.

It has been 2500 years since the brain was implicated in maternal mental illness, and yet we have much to learn. The following chapters will highlight what we do know. I will also briefly talk about different mental illnesses with motherhood which some of you may identify with, have experienced, or may be experiencing. If at any point you have questions about your mental health please speak to your physician, midwife or a trusted healthcare provider.

For those who are struggling, there is hope. Things are changing, and as the universal message from *Postpartum Support International* states: You are not alone, you are not to blame, and with help you will be well.

Chapter 17.

# Shouldn't I be happy?

"Being a mom makes me feel whole and like I understand the meaning of life... All I want to do is stare into my babies' eyes nonstop!" This is how Rebecca Romijn, a relatively famous American actress (most memorable for me as the supermodel boss in the television series *Ugly Betty*), spoke of her motherhood in an article in *Instyle* in 2009, shortly after her twins were born. It's the ideal motherhood isn't it—to now understand the meaning of life; and this from a mother of twins! You should see the photo that goes with this quote. She looks radiant holding her two adorable baby girls. For sure, it is normal to be happy to have children, but to say that you now understand the meaning of life (not to mention that Rebecca Romijn looked amazing a few months after having twins), how is this possible? Perhaps she had the finances for a nanny, babysitter or house cleaners, which we know can make things easier. Or she was putting on a brave face, as so many mothers do, and was suffering in silence. I only wish I looked that good with just one baby sitting on my knee... One thing I want to point out here is that we are surrounded by stories of the *bliss* with motherhood, that, in reality, may not be the whole story for that person. For many mothers, being a mom does not bring about an epiphany about the joy of life and that's completely normal.

Dr. Jacques Dayan, the first perinatal psychiatrist in France, begins his book *Les Baby Blues* by stating: "Pregnancy and motherhood are often privileged periods of fulfillment and joy. However, their idealization by society is likely to lead to the denial of the difficulties that many pregnant or postpartum women may encounter." This is so true.

When I was in graduate school, I read the memoir *Down Came the Rain: My Journey Through Postpartum Depression* (2005), by Brooke Shields, a famous US actor and model—perhaps most famous for her role in the movie *Blue Lagoon* (1980). This was probably the first pop-culture book on postpartum depression that became quite well known. This was in part because, on national television in the USA, Tom Cruise made some ridiculous claims about Brooke Shields struggles with postpartum depression and her antidepressant medication use, which brought to light the stigma new mothers face[201] (Tom later apologized). In her book, Brooke Shields' talks about her lack of feelings toward her new "angelic baby", and the guilt of not wanting to be near her lovely child. "My crying recommenced, and I started strongly believing that I couldn't be a mother... I remember looking out of the bedroom window and envisioning myself jumping. I concluded that it wouldn't be too effective, because we weren't high enough. This upset me even more...". These feelings of guilt, isolation, inadequacy and wanting to escape life happen to many new moms. I applaud Brooke Shields, and those others like her, that have shared their stories of what it is like to struggle with postpartum depression. With treatments they have recovered. There is hope.

Postpartum depression is probably the most well known and most talked about of the perinatal mental illnesses. It is often composed of a mix of symptoms that last for at least two weeks and occupy most of the day. These symptoms include persistent depressed mood and sadness, diminished pleasure in nearly all activities, changes in sleep patterns, changes in weight, fatigue, restlessness, feelings of worthlessness, poor concentration, anger, and reoccurring thoughts of death and suicide. In recent years the term "Perinatal Depression" has been more commonly used to classify depression during motherhood, both during pregnancy and the postpartum period (see DSM-5 criteria[202], the *Diagnostic and Statistical Manual of Mental Disorders*).

It should also be noted that suicide is the second leading cause of death in the perinatal period in France. A recent report[203] shows that "non-optimal care was present in 72% of cases and 91% of suicides were potentially preventable, preventability factors being a lack of multidisciplinary care and inadequate interaction between the patient and the care system." These findings are not new and we see that suicide is a leading cause of death in mothers in Canada, the UK and other countries studied to date. In fact, the heart-breaking results of a study in Canada[204] showed that "39% of the women who died by suicide during pregnancy or the postpartum period sought mental health support in the last month of their lives". Clearly the mental health care was too little, too late. We can do better! We need to improve how we screen and treat perinatal mental illness. I could probably write a few chapters about my thoughts on this but I'm going to stick to the brain, as I'm supposed to, and not let my blood boil too much with rage at how much we neglect maternal mental health, in particular.

I also want to note that some risk factors for developing perinatal depression include: a history of depression or anxiety, stress, domestic violence, poor social support, low household income, other health problems, discontinuing antidepressants, as well as biological factors, which I'll talk about below.

It is difficult to establish precise rates of perinatal depression due to how varied the illness can be from mother to mother, the stigma associated with not being happy about being a mother (and thus many suffer in silence), and the lack of consistent screening for psychiatric symptoms during pregnancy and the postpartum period. We very routinely screen for illnesses such as gestational diabetes, which occur in 7% of pregnant women[205], but we don't screen for depression and anxiety, which can be present at moderate to severe levels in an estimated 15% of mothers. This needs to change!

The World Health Organization (WHO) states[206]: "Worldwide, about 10% of pregnant women and 13% of women who have just given birth experience a mental disorder, primarily depression. In developing countries this is even higher, i.e. 15.6% during pregnancy and 19.8% after childbirth. In severe cases, mothers suffering might be so severe that they may even commit suicide. In addition, the affected mothers cannot function properly." And, of course, having a mental illness is not only terrible for a mother but can affect her child's development, as well as other relationships. The WHO goes on to clearly state that "maternal mental disorders are treatable. Effective interventions can be delivered even by well-trained non-specialist health providers.....". Perinatal mental illnesses are treatable. Perinatal depression is treatable. You will be well. There is hope. This is important to remember. Common treatments, to name a few, are psychotherapy, groups therapies, and antidepressant medications such as Zoloft (and YES you can take these during pregnancy and while breastfeeding, if anyone tells you differently, let me know and I'll give you the research supporting this. I've spent over a decade doing research in this area!).

## Neglected neurobiology

In 2017, I worked with my mentors and friends, Prof. Joseph Lonstein, at Michigan State University, and Prof. Alison Fleming, at the University of Toronto at Mississauga, to write a scientific review of the research on how perinatal depression and anxiety affect the brain of women. This work was published in *Trends in Neurosciences*[207], a prestigious journal from Cell Press Publishing Group.

Before I delve into our review, here is a bit of background on how I know Alison and Joe. Alison was on my master's thesis committee, years ago, at the University of Toronto. She is an international expert on the maternal brain. She is really the Mother of maternal brain research. Joe is a wonderful friend and collaborator, whom I met at a conference in probably my first year of graduate school. He also knows much about the maternal brain and, in particular, the neurobiology of maternal anxiety, which I'll talk more about in the next chapter.

When we started to review the scientific research on postpartum depression (as there is almost no work on depression and the brain in pregnancy), I was astonished by how little research there was on brain changes in mothers with postpartum depression. Until then, I had spent much of my research career focusing on how the hippocampus (a brain area important for memory and stress regulation) is affected by the combination of motherhood, stress and antidepressant medications, using rodent models. I hadn't followed the brain imaging data in women with postpartum depression as closely.

When we did review the brain imaging research in women with depressive symptoms during pregnancy or the postpartum period up to 2017, there were at best 25 published papers on the neurobiology of postpartum depression, and none on the neurobiology of depression in pregnancy.

Let's take a minute to put that in perspective and remember what the WHO said: "10% of pregnant women and 13% of women who have just given birth experience a mental disorder, primarily depression", with higher rates in developing countries. That's more women than will have gestational diabetes (7%) or probably most other medical issues related to childbirth. Yet, only 25 studies (and maybe a few more now) have looked at how perinatal depression affects a mother's brain. We should be outraged!

You may think that there just isn't so much research on brain changes in people with mental illness, but I did a quick estimate of research in this area for a talk I gave at a conference titled *Violences et soutiens a la maternite*[208] (*Violence and support in motherhood*), organized by Dr. Jacques Dayan in Rennes in 2020[209]. I went on Pubmed[210] (an indexing service internationally recognized as having a catalogue of the majority of medical research) and used search terms such as depression, MRI (magnetic resonance imaging) and brain. I found that there are 9085 published papers that have investigated depression, using brain imaging, in men and/or women. 9085! This number is compared to the 25 for women with postpartum depression. Incredible!

This is shocking and sad, given the prevalence of maternal mental illness and its effect on mother and child. Why then is our understanding of the neural bases of postpartum mood disorders relying on fewer than 25 published functional magnetic resonance imaging (fMRI) studies in postpartum women? It may be that postpartum depressive symptoms are so common (up to 80% of North American mothers have the postpartum "blues") that when they reach more severe clinical levels, these mental illnesses are considered normative rather than pathologic and, hence, have not received adequate attention from the scientific community. Another reason for this neglect, without a doubt, albeit political, is that these disorders are largely restricted to women, who for a long time have not been the focus of scientific inquiry or interest related to mental health and many other topics (although we now know that 4-6% of new fathers also experience post-birth depression, see Chapter 21). Or it may be that it has long been thought that these maternal mental illnesses were no different from these illnesses when they appear at other times in a women's life, and do not warrant a special status. However, this is not the case.

## The postpartum depressed brain

In our review of the scientific literature, we found that postpartum depression differs neurobiologically from depression at other times in a person's life. In postpartum depression and depression in non-parents there are similar brain areas involved, but how these brain areas are interconnected and respond to the environment differs.

Remember that I'm talking about brain imaging studies where moms are placed in the magnetic resonance imaging (MRI) scanner and brain activity is measured while they are either doing nothing, viewing a picture (usually of a baby) or listening to a baby cry. When presented with these cues (pictures or sounds) the brain will respond and measurements can be made of its general activity by looking at changes in blood flow (this is called fMRI, as mentioned in previous chapters).

Although not every brain area has been studied to date, we know from research in animal models, and other studies in humans, that there are core brain areas implicated in depression and motherhood. Researchers have then investigated how these brain areas may respond differently when a mother has depressive symptoms or has been diagnosed with postpartum depression.

To date, depression has been associated with alterations in activity of cortical and subcortical brain areas, such as the anterior cingulate cortex, the insula, the orbital frontal cortex, the amygdala, the striatum, and the hippocampus. These brain areas all play a role in coordinating maternal behaviors. Our review of the literature also showed that the connectivity between different brain areas could be disrupted in mothers with depression, showing a wide range of brain changes that exist with postpartum depression.

Of course, as no single brain area is responsible for one behavioral outcome, it is important to highlight that alterations in activation of brain areas during postpartum depression likely alter key neural networks associated with maternal care, empathy, stress regulation, motivation and reward, emotional regulation, and decision making.

One brain area that has received much of the limited research on postpartum depression in women is the amygdala. The amygdala is important for processing of emotional stimuli and makes vital connections throughout the brain. Given that one of the features of postpartum depression is lack of pleasure, recent work by Alison's group[211] explored mothers' brain response specifically to positive infant pictures (a baby

134

smiling) and to other positive stimuli. In this study, the authors showed that, when compared to mothers without depression, mothers with clinically determined postpartum depression have an overall *enhanced* response in the right amygdala to positive infant photos and positive non-infant photos, but *decreased* connectivity bilaterally between the amygdala and the insular cortex, when they viewed pictures of their own versus another smiling baby. Furthermore, decreasing the connectivity between the amygdala and insular cortex was associated with increasing symptoms of depression and anxiety. These differences were evident only for infant stimuli and did not apply to all positive emotional stimuli. Moreover, the strength of the connectivity between the amygdala and the insular cortex was related to how a mother interacted with her baby, as measured by maternal sensitivity in mother-infant interactions. Thus, mothers with postpartum depression showed altered brain responses and connectivity between brain regions that were associated with their depressive symptoms and their interactions with their babies.

Whether these brain changes occur before postpartum depression, or after, has yet to be determined, but I suspect both the psychological changes and neurobiological changes parallel each other over time. I also want to point out again, that depression in pregnancy is common and likely involves similar brain areas, but potentially with different responses to cues. Hopefully future research will shed light on this.

## Perinatal Depression vs Major Depressive Disorder

As already mentioned, Perinatal Depression is not simply Major Depressive Disorder. Although postpartum depression and major depression share many symptom characteristics, with the exception of the infant/family focus and the perinatal timing of postpartum depression, they have different neurobiological activation profiles. For example, women with postpartum depression show *decreased* activation in the amygdala and striatum in response to non-infant related emotional cues such as emotional words, whereas individuals with major depression show *increased* activation in the amygdala and striatum in response to similar emotional cues. Therefore, it is not possible to simply extrapolate conclusions from neuroimaging studies of major depression to postpartum depression, because it will overlook the unique effects of motherhood on brain regions that play a vital role in mothering.

At the time we wrote our review[212], there was no research directly comparing brain changes in mothers and non-mothers, which would have provided some indication of the specific brain changes that occur with postpartum depression. However, in 2019, Aya Dudin, a student of Alison's, published a study[213] on how the amygdala responds (using fMRI) to a picture of a baby smiling or a picture of nature, in mothers with postpartum depression and women (non-mothers) with major depression. It is the first comparison of its kind in perinatal depression research in women. Aya found that moms with postpartum depression have an enhanced amygdala response to a picture of a smiling infant compared to other mothers, and also when compared to women with major depression (non-mothers) and women (non-mothers) without depression. These results provide compelling evidence that brain activity changes are unique in postpartum mental illnesses, and thus more tailored treatments should be developed to target these unique brain changes.

## What do hormones have to do with it?

Remember in the last chapter I mentioned that Hippocrates, 2500 years ago, speculated that hormones (he didn't call them that during that time) can have an impact in the brain and result in postpartum depression. Smart man. Great observation. But 2500 years later we're at the same place. We know that hormones, such as estradiol and cortisol, are important in depression during pregnancy and the postpartum period but we don't have a clear idea of how. I've recently reviewed the literature on this[214] and it suggests that in some women the decrease in estradiol levels at the time of birth can be a trigger for postpartum depression. In other women, the rise in cortisol levels in the blood (cortisol is commonly thought of as a "stress" hormone) can be associated with depression in pregnancy. Recent research suggests that there is a time course in the relationship between cortisol concentrations and postpartum depressed mood, with higher cortisol concentrations being associated with depressed mood in women during the first week postpartum, but lower cortisol concentrations being associated with depressed mood weeks or months later[215]. But really, we don't know all the biological factors that contribute to perinatal depression. I suspect it is a mix of hormones, genetics, and environmental factors that play a role. More research is needed.

## If only I knew...

It is abundantly clear that we need to increase our understanding of the neurobiology of perinatal depression and how maternal mental illness can disrupt the maternal care-giving network, the mother-infant dyad and the family. But maybe, more so, we need to share what we do know about how the brain changes with perinatal depression and with motherhood, in general.

I say this because women want to know. In an article in the *Boston Globe* in 2018[216], Chelsea Conaboy, a journalist and author based in the USA, wrote: "What I didn't know then—what I wish I had known then—was that I was in the midst of the most rapid and dramatic neurobiological change of my adult life. The unmooring I felt, and that so many new mothers feel, likely was at least in part a manifestation of structural and functional brain changes, handed down through the millennia by mothers past and intended to mold me into a fiercely protective, motivated caregiver, focused on my baby's survival and long-term well-being." I spoke to Chelsea, and I was amazed to hear how much relief she got from knowing that her brain was changing with motherhood. Since then, mothers and health care professionals who work with new moms have told me how important it has been for them and their clients to know that the brain changes with motherhood. For maternal mental health, it's essential.

In the summer 2020, I spoke with Emma Jane Unsworth, an award-winning novelist in the UK, for the book she was writing about her own experience with postpartum (postnatal) depression. In May of 2021, her book titled *After the Storm: Postnatal Depression and the Utter Weirdness of New Motherhood*[217] was published and I highly recommend reading it. One thing that she talks about in her book is that if only she'd known..." "If I'd known there were massive brain changes afoot—if I'd known that unfamiliar emotions are part of a *healthy* experience of new motherhood—it might not have felt as much like my fault, or my failing when they tipped over into something else..."

I wish she had known.

Chapter 18.

# Good moms have scary thoughts

A few years before I had kids, while I was still doing my doctoral research, I remember talking with a friend of mine, a mom of a 2 or 3-year-old at the time (I can't remember the exact details), and she told me this "you will probably think of how your child will be harmed 100 times a day, and that's normal". I was surprised by this statement as I hadn't heard anyone talk about this until then.

At that time, I was studying the maternal brain but I was studying brain changes related to memory and not anxiety. I remember not really understanding what she was talking about. How could I? I wasn't a mom then and I didn't have many friends who were parents. I didn't know what it was like to worry about a child. What I did know was that this was important information to file away for future—it's normal to be anxious and worry when you have a baby.

*Good moms have scary thoughts*[218] is the title of a book by Karen Kleiman, a therapist and writer, specializing in perinatal mental health. Coincidentally Karen Kleiman supported Alanis Morrisette when she struggled with what she calls "postpartum activity"—"it's depression, anxiety, a lot of hormones stuff and a lot of neurobiological stuff".[219]

Alanis is Canadian and I've been a fan since my teen years so when she started talking about her postpartum activity with each of her three children I nearly became a groupie. Her album, which came out in 2020, has a song related to her postpartum experience: *Diagnosis*. Listen to it, if you haven't already. I also love *Ablaze*, a song for her children.

Good moms have scary thoughts. It's a fact. Dads have them too. In her book, Karen Kleiman writes that "90% of moms will have scary, intrusive thoughts about their baby and themselves". These thoughts can be on a range of different themes. Some of them will be about the baby being hurt or dying: "what if he/she doesn't wake up?". Others may focus on how the mother (or parent) herself may be a danger for her child: "what if I drop my baby?" or "what if I let the pram go from the top of a hill?", to name a few. These thoughts are often scary but fleeting. And they are just thoughts, that's the part that's difficult to understand sometimes. Thoughts don't mean actions are inevitable. The thoughts play on things that could happen, but most likely never will.

In an article published in the *British Journal of General Practice*[220], the psychologist and researcher Peter Lawrence advises telling parents the following in order to normalize intrusive anxious thoughts:

- Intrusive thoughts or images of causing harm to one's infant are common in the general population.

- Experiencing the intrusive thoughts makes them no more likely to harm their infant intentionally than any other parent is to harm their own infant intentionally.

- There is no need to avoid triggers or situations that give rise to the intrusive thoughts or images. Avoiding them actually tends to increase the frequency of the thoughts and/or images.

This may be easier said than done, but the fact of the matter is that intrusive thoughts and worry are very common and normal during late pregnancy and the postpartum period. Thoughts are just thoughts.

Anxiety can come in many forms and, to some degree, is healthy. We want to be on guard to protect and care for our child. It's important that we anticipate what could happen to them. We're biologically "wired" to want our child to survive, so some worries are likely necessary for our child's wellbeing. The problem is when these worries and fears start to take over our lives and consume us.

Many new parents struggle with anxiety that goes beyond this normative "healthy" level, but often they suffer in silence, scared to admit their fears, scared they will be judged, and terrified something is wrong with them.

## Ordinary insanity

We don't talk enough about anxiety disorders and motherhood. We probably don't talk enough about anxiety disorders, in general. It is estimated that 30% of the general population will have an anxiety disorder at one point in their lives. That's nearly 1 in 3 people. Think about that. I was one of them. I had severe intrusive thoughts near the end of my doctoral thesis that became incredibly debilitating for a time. With therapy, perseverance, and learning how to better manage my stress I was able to learn how to control these thoughts.

Fortunately, I didn't have debilitating intrusive thoughts during pregnancy or the postpartum period. I did have all sorts of thoughts that centered around "what ifs" ("What if I did this or that to my baby?"). None of these thoughts left me in a panic or tears because I had learned how to manage them, take a breath and let them go. But they were there, they are still there sometimes. For example, I've thought things like "the kids shouldn't have the room at the top of the stairs because they would be the first ones to be attacked if someone broke into the house at night." Is this normal? Probably. Can I see that it's a bit far-fetched? Yes. Do either of my kids sleep in the room at the top of the stairs? No. I wouldn't call myself a "helicopter mom", but I do have anxious thoughts, like most of us, that sometimes come out of nowhere and are a bit above and beyond. I can let them go (after a time), because I've learned what works for me, but for some new moms a cycle of worry is impossible to stop.

Why don't we talk about perinatal anxiety more? I think one reason is that it often occurs with depression or may actually occur before depression, but not have been detected early on.

I asked Dr. Nichole Fairbrother, Clinical Associate Professor of Psychiatry at the University of British Columbia and Registered Psychologist, an expert in perinatal anxiety, about this. Why don't we talk more about postpartum anxiety (or perinatal anxiety)? We have public figures talking about postpartum depression (which often includes anxiety symptoms) but why not about perinatal anxiety? She told me this: "This is such a great question. For some reason it has been difficult to get it taken as seriously as depression. It's better now, but still far behind. What's odd about that is that perinatal anxiety disorders have a prevalence that is about double that of major depression (with perinatal onset):... It's frustrating." She goes on to mention that if you ask those who work with mothers about what mothers are talking about it, it is most often anxiety, not depression.

I've also been trying to think of a celebrity who has shared their experience with perinatal anxiety and I can't actually think of one. I googled "postpartum anxiety celebrity" and the first hits that came up were for celebrities with postpartum depression. It's important to be talking about postpartum depression to decrease the stigma, but I think it's time we start to talk about perinatal anxiety. This illness can be just as debilitating as perinatal depression.

Recent research states[221] that clinical levels of anxiety exist in 13-21% of pregnant women and 11-17% of postpartum women. That's nearly 1 in every 5 moms. That's significant. Think about 5 of your friends who are mothers. One of them will have significant anxiety—probably at a clinical level. The unfortunate thing is that anxiety is often seen as part of perinatal depression. In the US and Canada, the word "postpartum" is commonly used to refer to postpartum depression and/or anxiety. Every mom has postpartum—it's a time period not a disorder.

In 2020, Sarah Menkedick wrote a book about "fear and the silent crisis of motherhood in America" titled *Ordinary Insanity*. I spoke with Sarah about the maternal brain while she was writing her book and I listened to the audiobook shortly after it was released. She shares her experiences with obsessive compulsive disorder (OCD) as a new mom and the stories of other women who struggled with fear and anxiety as mothers. She writes "I couldn't separate it [fear and anxiety] out from the set of 'normal', culturally and medically and socially solicited behaviors appropriate to new motherhood. I couldn't draw a line where my fear crossed over into the darker territory of illness."

## Bad thoughts

I've been using "anxiety" as a general term, but there are different anxiety disorders which involve anxiety-related symptoms. Anxiety itself refers to "anticipation of future threat[222]", which is rather general. There are also ongoing classification discussions around what is an anxiety disorder, but that is beyond the focus of this chapter. When we are talking about clinical levels of perinatal anxiety, research has found that generalized anxiety disorder, panic disorder, obsessive compulsive disorder[223] (OCD), and specific phobia may be the most common types[224]. There is no perinatal specific anxiety disorder. These disorders rely on the classification of anxiety disorders that happen at any time in life. This makes sense, but often the specific anxieties in the perinatal period are focused on the child, which makes them unique.

In brief, generalized anxiety disorder at any time in life includes the presence of excessive anxiety and worry about a variety of topics, events or activities. This anxiety and worry is very difficult to control and occurs more often than not for at least six months, and is clearly excessive. Panic disorder includes sudden attacks of fear where there is an intense rush of mental and physical symptoms: shortness of breath, nausea, dizziness, sweating etc. Obsessive compulsive disorder (OCD) typically includes "recurring, unwanted thoughts, ideas or sensations (obsessions) that make one feel driven to do something repetitively (compulsions)[225]". A specific phobia "is an intense, irrational fear of something that poses little or no actual danger[226]."

This is a brief summary of these common anxiety disorders during the perinatal period but I want to point out that the diagnosis criteria for these disorders is more complex than what is stated here, so please see your general practitioner if you feel that you may be struggling with one of these anxiety disorders.

## Brain changes with anxiety—playing out of tune

"In the weeks after my first son was born", wrote Chelsea Conaboy[227], "I squandered hours of precious sleep leaning over his bassinet to check that he was still breathing, or Googling potential dangers that seemed to grow into monstrous reality by the blue light of my smartphone. Among them: The lead paint my husband and I had discovered recently—a real but manageable risk—had turned our new home into a hazard zone. I cleaned our floors incessantly but still imagined a cartoonish cloud of poison dust following us as I carried the baby, so tiny and fragile, from room to room... . I feared that something deep within me—my disposition, my way of seeing the world, myself—had been altered. In truth, something very foundational had changed: my brain."

How does your brain change with perinatal anxiety? That is the big, unanswered question. We know that many life factors contribute to an increased risk of developing an anxiety disorder during pregnancy or the postpartum period. Factors such as having had an anxiety disorder or another mental illness previously, birth complications, low social support, low income and low levels of education can increase the risk that you may develop an anxiety disorder when becoming a mother[228]. And remember, this is increased risk, not a guarantee that this will happen. When it comes to the biology behind perinatal anxiety disorders we don't know as much, especially when we are talking about neurobiology. This is often due to the fact that perinatal depression and anxiety are investigated together under the term "perinatal depression" even though many women will have anxiety without depression and vice versa.

Let's talk a bit more about perinatal anxiety and its effect on the brain. As I mentioned in the last chapter, I've been fortunate to work with Prof. Joseph Lonstein, Professor of Psychology at Michigan State University, and an expert in the neurobiology of perinatal anxiety. We talked in the first episode of my podcast Mommy Brain Revisited[229] about perinatal anxiety and here are some key points from that episode. As with perinatal depression, there are similar brain areas involved in anxiety, regardless of whether anxiety occurs in the perinatal period or not. It's how these brain areas are functioning, or how the neurochemicals of these brain areas work, that is important.

In general, the "classic anxiety network" in the brain focuses on the amygdala, a brain area I've mentioned quite a bit. It plays a primary role in fear and anxiety (as well as emotions and many other things studied to date). The amygdala doesn't act alone, the BNST or bed nucleus of the stria terminalis, which is located above the amygdala, seems to monitor threats and let the amygdala know what it should respond to. Areas on the "top", or cortex, of the brain are also important, as they "decide" whether something is worth worrying about or not. They can "calm" the amygdala before it sends output to the periaqueductal grey (PAG), located in the "lower" parts of the brain, to notify it of generating an anxiety response or not. There are other brain areas involved, of course, but the brain areas I've mentioned here are key brain areas and give you an idea of the complexity of this network.

Apart from the brain areas involved, there are a number of neurochemical changes that take place to generate an anxiety response. This work has been predominately done in animal models but similar neurochemicals are also involved in anxiety in humans. Joe states that there is "an orchestra of neurochemicals that have to work together to get the typical anxiety decreasing effects of motherhood. GABA, serotonin, oxytocin, progesterone, estradiol. Small manipulations in any system can change anxiety in the mother. How your brain manages anxiety is like an orchestra that works together. Each system is changing in different ways, at different times across the peripartum period, and collectively they are working to get a healthy affective state that is ideal to care for the young." He goes on to say that "there is no one neurochemical that is driving perinatal anxiety disorders". There are many intertwined and acting together.

In women, only a few studies of brain activity exist that were done in the context of perinatal anxiety[230]. Work out of Prof. Alison Fleming's lab[231] using fMRI techniques, found that activity[232] in the amygdala of mothers was higher while they viewed pictures of their own infant or another infant if the mothers were more anxious generally (as evidenced by anxiety trait questionnaires). Consistent with this result, the women with high anxiety also expressed lower positive feelings about their own infant. Mothers with lower levels of anxiety showed an increase in amygdala response only when viewing their own infant.

This same research group[233] later reported that mothers with high trait anxiety (but not necessarily depression) showed lower functional connectivity between the amygdala and insular cortex. The insula is involved in many functions including social processing of emotions such as empathy, suggesting the amygdala-insula pathway as the basis of anxious mothers' reduced caregiving sensitivity.

Using electroencephalogram (EEG) techniques to investigate brain activity (or brain "waves"), Dr. Helena Rutherford and colleagues at Yale University[234] showed that in mothers with higher levels of anxiety, brain activity is increased in response to neutral, unambiguous infant faces (not crying, not smiling), compared to mothers with lower levels of anxiety. It is interesting to note that the two groups of mothers show similar brain activity when they are exposed to a sad infant face. This research suggests that in mothers with high levels of anxiety there is a bias toward interpreting threat in an infant's face, which likely further increases feelings of anxiety, creating a vicious cycle.

## Are hormones to blame?

As with perinatal depression, it is commonly thought that particularly large or rapid fluctuations in steroid or peptide hormones across the peripartum period act centrally to trigger perinatal anxiety[235]. This may be true for some women, who, for mostly unknown reasons, may be susceptible to the negative effects of changes in circulating hormones. Unfortunately, while there is evidence supporting this hypothesis for the hormone changes in anxiety and depression across the menstrual cycle, there is little research supporting the role of hormones in anxiety and depression during the perinatal period. Hopefully one day we will be able to better understand the hormonal and neurochemical alterations that happen with anxiety disorders in mothers.

But know this: there are brain changes with perinatal anxiety disorders. Even though we don't know exactly what is going on in the brain, there are treatment options to help you manage anxiety. If you have difficulties, talk to your health care provider or look at *Postpartum Support International*. You are not alone. With support, you will be well.

## Beyond scary thoughts

Before I leave this chapter, I want to talk briefly about another disorder that happens, much less commonly, in the postpartum period than depression and anxiety, that can also include anxiety—but in a different way. I'm talking about Postpartum Psychosis.

Postpartum psychosis occurs in the 1-2 of every 1000 birthing mothers during the postpartum period. The leading organization with information on postpartum psychosis—*Action on Postpartum Psychosis* (APP)—states that "Postpartum psychosis[236] is a severe, but treatable, form of mental illness that occurs after having a baby. It can happen 'out of the blue' to women without previous experience of mental illness." There are some mothers (women with a history of bipolar disorder, for example) who are at a much higher risk. Postpartum psychosis normally begins in the first few days to weeks after childbirth. It can get worse very quickly and should always be treated as a medical emergency. Most women need to be treated with medication and admitted to hospital.

Postpartum psychosis can consist of a variety of symptoms, including anxiety and depression. It also must include (according to APP), "Strange beliefs that could not be true (delusions); hearing, seeing, feeling or smelling things that are not there (hallucinations); high mood with loss of touch with reality (mania); severe confusion". You may think it's difficult to differentiate whether a scary thought (as mentioned above in the case of anxiety) is a delusion, but it's not. The difference is that a delusion or hallucination feels true and real to the person having them. It's not something that could happen, it is happening.

Often, not feeling the need to sleep is an early sign that something could be wrong. This symptom, coupled with other symptoms such as racing thoughts, paranoid feelings, feeling very energetic, believing the baby is connected to God or the devil, believing in "signs" from the world around you, are signs to talk to a health care professional. This is a life threatening disorder with 4-5% of women dying by suicide or committing infanticide.

Today, although it is a relatively rare disorder, there is some work on the neurobiological changes related to postpartum psychosis. This is a mental illness that can't be easily studied in animal models. It's necessary that we rely on human research, which is incredibly difficult! Imagine asking a new mother to participate in a study or lie in an MRI scanner when she is afraid people may be out to get her or her baby, or she is too restless to sit down. It's probably the most difficult disorder to study. Fortunately, Prof. Paola Dazzan, Professor of Neurobiology of Psychosis and Vice Dean International at the Institute of Psychiatry, Psychology & Neuroscience at King's College London, has taken up the challenge! Her research focuses on how postpartum psychosis affects the brain. She's also met with Kate, Princess of Wales, to talk about her research. How impressive!

I talked with Paola about her research on my podcast[237]. In her research on postpartum psychosis[238], she found that mothers with a recent episode of postpartum psychosis had a smaller anterior cingulate gyrus, superior temporal gyrus and parahippocampal gyrus (the first two areas are located in the limbic region and the third in the temporal lobe), compared to mothers at risk to develop postpartum psychosis but who did not develop it[239]. These brain areas are involved in regulation of emotions, empathy, as well as decision making. They are also involved in emotion perception. The mothers who were at risk, but didn't have a psychotic episode, had a larger volume of the frontal gyrus compared to mothers not at risk, which may be a protective factor that requires more investigation.

She also mentioned that, although there are similar brain areas involved in postpartum psychosis and in psychosis at other times in life, the way these brain areas are connected is different in mothers with postpartum psychosis. Specifically, her research[240] has found that the dorsal lateral prefrontal cortex (a brain area typically associated with executive functions such as working memory and selective attention) is more connected with other brain areas in mothers who have postpartum psychosis than in non-mothers with psychosis at other times in life—where the dorsal lateral prefrontal cortex is less connected with other brain areas.

Here again, research is pointing to a unique neurobiology of perinatal mental illness, similar to what I talked about with postpartum depression in the previous chapter. Understanding these unique brain changes with perinatal mental illness may be a key to understanding which women are at risk for postpartum psychosis and other maternal mental illnesses.

In summary, postpartum psychosis and all maternal mental illnesses are biological disorders linked to changes in the brain. It's been 2500 years that we have speculated that hormones and the brain are responsible for perinatal mental illness. Let's please not let another 2500 years pass before we know how.

Chapter 19.

# The battlefield
# of birth

Over the last few years, obstetric violence in France has been in the news nationally and internationally. Is it because France has a higher rate of obstetric violence than other countries or that more people are talking about it? It's hard to say. The thing is, it's real and needs to be talked about (and for the record, I don't know what it's like to give birth in France. I had one of my children in Belgium and the other in the USA).

By definition, obstetric violence is the abuse of women during pregnancy, childbirth, and the postpartum period. *Alliance Francophone pour l'Accouchement Respecté* (AFAR[241]) (French Alliance for Respect during Birth) states: "Gynecological and obstetrical violence is any behavior, act, word or omission by health care personnel that is not medically justified or is done without the free and informed consent of a pregnant woman, parturient or new mother." Inappropriate or sexist behaviors are also identified.

In 2020, I was part of a conference titled *Violences et soutiens a la maternite*[242] where I spoke of the neglected neurobiology of maternal mental illness. I also met Sonia Bisch, the founder of Stop aux Violences Obstétricales et Gynécologiques (StopVOG). For her, obstetrical abuse is a major cause of suicide in mothers for whom the traumatic episode during labor is unbearable (suicide is the second leading cause of maternal death in France[243]). She may be right, I don't know. I know that trauma during birth can affect mental health. It is estimated that 30%

of women have had a traumatic event during childbirth. And between 3% of "low-risk" and 19% of "high-risk" women (e.g., who have a cesarean section) will develop childbirth-related posttraumatic stress disorder (PTSD), with no difference in rates between home and hospital births[244] (at least in the Netherlands, where this study was conducted).

PTSD after childbirth also has strong links to postpartum depression (72% in some studies[245]). PTSD "occurs after experiencing or witnessing an event that has induced a threat of death or dying, serious injury or physical threat. During childbirth, some women may experience a real or perceived threat to their physical integrity, their life and/or the life of the child. The symptoms of PTSD are grouped into four categories: re-experiencing, avoidance, negative cognitions and mood, and hyperarousal. All of these symptoms must be present for at least one month and interfere with social and work life.[246]"

## Childbirth related PTSD

The development of PTSD after birth depends on a number of factors—biological, social and psychological. It exists, and obstetric violence is a contributor. Obstetric violence, itself, exists for a number of reasons related to education (or lack thereof), but also sexism, racism and classism.... these are not excuses and need to be addressed. Identifying the causes of obstetric violence will lead to ways to prevent this abuse.

Prof. Antje Horsch, at the University of Lausanne, and Prof. Susan Garthus-Niegal, at the University of Dresden, are experts in this area with many publications on PTSD related to childbirth. I met Susan in 2017 at the *European Psychiatric Association* annual meeting, where we had a long talk about her research on interventions for birth trauma—a fascinating topic I'll talk about below. Research they have done together and separately is showing that PTSD related to birth can affect both parents (much less in fathers[247]), is related to prenatal insomnia[248], can be reduced by pain medications during birth[249], affects bonding with baby[250], is related to decreased breastfeeding rates[251], and can be effectively screened for by using the *City Birth Trauma Scale* questionnaire. I think you get the point that these two are experts. I also hope you see that we have tools to aid in preventing and detecting birth trauma. The biggest "tool" to decrease birth trauma will be when health care providers improve their practices to engage the birthing person and see her as a key player in birth. Perhaps this will be best done with more research devoted to understanding the birthing process and implementing this information into standard health care training.

## Trauma, birth and the maternal brain

The link between birth trauma and the brain is something we know very little about. In an article titled *PTSD and Obstetric Violence* in *Midwifery Today* in 2013[252], Dr. Ibone Olzo Fernandez, a Perinatal Psychiatrist, researcher, writer and CEO of the *European Institute of Perinatal Mental Health*, wrote: "It is possible that abusive care can have a bigger impact when it happens during childbirth, a time when the maternal brain is imprinted with specific neurohormones that make it ready for initiating attachment." Unfortunately, we don't know how trauma during birth can change the parental brain. Brain imaging studies (fMRI) have been conducted on maternal PTSD (not related to birth) and its impact on the maternal brain. Neural activation in mothers with interpersonal violence-related PTSD[253] shows that[254] when watching videos of young children (their own or an unknown one) during separation or free play, they show increased activity in the insula and dorsolateral prefrontal cortex, as well as decreased activity in the cingulate, hippocampus, and medial prefrontal cortex. These patterns of brain activity were associated with mothers' reported feelings of stress or dissociative symptoms (e.g., memory loss, feeling detached, feeling fuzzy). What exactly does this mean? As a recent study[255] nicely summarized: "Mothers with interpersonal violence-related PTSD activated an "uncontrolled" fear circuit that was associated with higher subjective stress ratings. The circuit described included increased activity...It has been suggested that hyperactivity in the fear circuit associated with interpersonal violence PTSD may induce a reduction in maternal emotional availability..."

Other authors have reported that a mother's unresolved childhood trauma blunts her amygdala response to infant distress,[256] that a mother's current socioeconomic disadvantages are "associated with attenuated amygdala responses to positive infant faces, but increased amygdala responses to negative infant faces,"[257] and that a mother exposed to chronic war-related trauma has altered neural capacity to integrate the sensory and affective components of empathy[258].

The point here is that trauma and stress can impact the maternal (and likely paternal) brain, whether it's early life trauma or current trauma and stress. I suspect the impact of PTSD related to birth on the maternal brain is significant, affecting key brain areas important for emotional regulation (amygdala), memory (hippocampus) and empathy (insula).

## *Tetris* for treating trauma?

One promising intervention for decreasing the impact of birth trauma on the maternal brain is to play *Tetris*. Too easy, right? In fact, research on *Tetris* for the treatment of PTSD, in general, has been around for a few years. I first heard about this work from Dr. Susan Garthus-Niegal and was fascinated by it. It's such a simple and safe intervention, why not? In a recent study by Dr. Antje Horsch[259] and her colleagues, they found that if mothers play *Tetris* for 15 minutes within 6 hours of an emergency c-section (in addition to normal interventions and care), the mothers had significantly fewer intrusive traumatic memories over the following week compared to moms who simply have the normal interventions and care. Wow!

How is this possible? From previous research, the idea is that playing the game interferes with your brain's ability to make a memory for the traumatic event, likely affecting the hippocampus. The memory will still be there but it won't be stored as such a traumatic event. I suspect this is because the storage is interrupted by *Tetris* and thus there is a decrease in the details of the traumatic memory, decreasing the risk of developing PTSD. Further research is needed on this but I see no harm in a little post-birth *Tetris* anytime, don't you?

What about me? Although I wouldn't say either of my births were traumatic, and they definitely didn't have any form of obstetric violence, they both were incredibly intense—a story for another time. However, I do remember that after the swift and intense birth of my son (my second and last)—a birth where I didn't think I could do it in the end—I was done. Done with birth. While my midwife was stitching my 2nd degree tear,[260] I joked with her and said, "you can sew it shut down there". That birth did me in and it took nearly 7 years to entertain the thought of having a third, which I won't be doing, not because of the thought of giving birth again (that has left) but because I'm happy with two.

Chapter 20.

# When the brain can't finish what it started

I first remember learning about miscarriage from my mom. If I remember correctly, she had a miscarriage before she gave birth to me, her 4th child. When she was pregnant with me things also didn't go as smoothly as anticipated and she required a fair amount of bed rest. Nonetheless, I arrived. Baby number 4. The last one. I guess I'd be called a rainbow baby today—a baby born after miscarriage (or stillbirth)—"something beautiful after a scary and dark experience[261]".

The topic of pregnancy loss, both miscarriage and stillbirth, has received increasing press over the past few years. In the fall of 2020, the celebrity Chrissy Teigen, who lost her little boy Jack at 20 weeks of gestation, wrote on her Instagram account: "We are in shock, and feel the kind of pain we've only heard about, the kind of pain we've never felt before...". Miscarriage, which is often defined as spontaneous pregnancy loss up to 20 weeks gestation, is something we don't talk enough about. It is almost seen as a kind of normal thing. It definitely is common in the first trimester (it is estimated to affect 1 in 7 women). But just because it's common doesn't mean it doesn't leave emotional and physical scars. Stillbirth often refers to pregnancy loss after 20 weeks gestation, but this criterion varies between countries. In France, stillbirth is considered after 22 weeks of gestation, or a birthweight of 500g or more. It is estimated that 9.2 of every 1000 births are stillbirths in France[262].

## Impact on mental health

Those are the numbers, but what about the impact of pregnancy loss on the mother? As you can imagine, it can be devastating. I remember the first time I knew someone who had suffered a stillbirth. It was the sister-in-law of a good friend. I had met her while she was pregnant. It was her first baby, a boy. She was glowing. My friend called me the day her sister-in-law went into labor to tell me that the baby didn't have a heartbeat. The baby was dead. The labor and birth had to proceed and the end result was a beautiful baby boy who was not meant for this earth. But the mother's body was ready to care for this little one. I imagine in the initial days and weeks, the "left over" physical effects of pregnancy and birth were a constant reminder of the loss of her baby, of her hopes and dreams. Her breasts were producing milk, her lochia was discharging for days, her pregnancy weight was there, and her brain—a brain primed to mother—could not.

Given the extent of this suffering, regardless of the stage of pregnancy, it is surprising how little we know about how this affects the brain. We certainly know that pregnancy loss, especially stillbirth, has a significant impact on a mother's (and father's) mental health. In a meta-analysis published in 2016[263], researchers found that still birth could have a pervasive impact on many areas of life—it "can have devastating psychological, physical and social costs, with ongoing effects on interpersonal relationships and subsequently born children".

To further clarify the impact of stillbirth on mental health, a study published in 2019, using health linked data of over one million women in Florida State[264] (8292 women with stillborn babies and 1,194,758 women with live-born babies), found that within one year of stillbirth, 4.0% of the women experiencing a stillbirth had an Emergency Department encounter or "inpatient admission for a psychiatric indication", compared to 1.6% of women after a live birth. The risk of severe psychiatric disorder was nearly 2.5 times higher after stillbirth compared to live birth. The authors report that the highest risk for psychiatric illness was within four months of stillbirth, although the risk remained high during the 4-12 months after delivery.

Early pregnancy loss, or miscarriage (before 14 weeks gestation), may not be as impactful emotionally, but it is not without its emotional impact. Many women experience post-traumatic stress, anxiety and depression after early pregnancy loss. In a study published in 2020[265], women who had experienced early pregnancy loss were questioned about their mental health, one, three, and nine months after experiencing their miscarriage. A few hundred women participated in the study. The authors of the study report that in the month after their early pregnancy loss, 29% of women met the criteria for post-traumatic stress. Nine months later, 18% of these women still had post-traumatic stress symptoms. When looking at anxiety symptoms with early pregnancy loss, 24% of women had moderate to severe anxiety a month later, and 17% were still experiencing moderate to severe anxiety symptoms nine months later. Moderate to severe depressive symptoms were evident in 11% of women, one month later, with 6% having symptoms nine months after the loss. The conclusions of this study were that many women experiencing early pregnancy loss have post-traumatic stress symptoms that can last for months. In addition, compared to women who are pregnant, women who experience early pregnancy loss were twice as likely to have moderate to severe anxiety and more than 3 times as likely to have moderate to severe depression, compared to women with ongoing pregnancies (with a healthy baby). Pregnancy loss, at any stage of gestation, can have an impact on a woman's mental health.

I also want to point out that the impact of pregnancy loss on mental health is often considered or diagnosed as grief and not postpartum depression or anxiety. In a article published in 2021[266] we reviewed the impact of pregnancy loss on the maternal brain with a focus on oxytocin and stress-reactivity systems. We state that "psychological symptoms following the loss of a loved one can range from feeling insecure, agitated, aggressive, anxious and having difficulties accepting the loss, to depressive states that can lead in 7% to 10% of the bereaved population to Prolonged Grief Disorder (PGD) i.e., when the symptoms last more than 6 months. However, in bereaved parents up to 94% of parents will develop PGD." Here, we are not necessarily just talking about pregnancy loss, but it gives you an idea of how much losing a child can impact a parent—often far more than losing another loved one.

## How is the brain impacted?

The short answer is we don't know much. I actually "fell" into this area of research when I was doing my doctoral thesis. In my studies on maternal memory and hippocampal neurogenesis in the maternal brain, I had a group of rat moms where I removed their offspring within 24 hours of giving birth. This was done to understand if it was pregnancy alone or the interaction with offspring that was important for memory outcomes and brain changes. In this study, there were five groups of rats: non-moms, first-time moms, second-time moms, moms that had their pups removed after birth and non-moms exposed to offspring. In this first study, with a "grieving mom"[267], I was looking at memory and motherhood after the time of weaning. As with other rat studies I've talked about, working and reference memory was investigated using an eight-arm radial maze (see Part I). For a reminder, this maze has a small circle in the middle with eight arms projecting outwards and rats must remember which four arms have a food reward. This test is done every day for a couple of weeks and the rats get really good at it.

When I did this study with the mother rats that had their offspring removed (modelling stillbirth), they could not do the task. Five weeks later, these "grieving mothers" failed to perform the task on more days than the other female rats, and they had significantly poorer memory compared to all the other rats. I was shocked when I saw this data. I hadn't really thought about pregnancy loss before, especially in my research.

The obvious next step with this research was to see if moms who had offspring removed permanently shortly after birth showed anxiety or depressive-type behaviors[268]. In animal models, we use different tests for this. For anxiety, I used a maze which is a raised plus, called the Elevated Plus Maze. The maze has four arms that are a few centimeters wide and about 60cm long: two arms have high walls and two arms have no walls. The idea is, the rat who is more anxious will spend more time in the arms with high walls than in the arms with no walls. We can't measure depression, per se, in animals but we can measure behaviors that are associated with depression such as "giving up" or lack of motivation, anhedonia, etc. In this study, I used a forced swim test which is a test where a rat (a natural swimmer) is put in a cylinder of warm water that they can't escape from. The amount of time they spend "giving up" or floating is an indication of depressive-like behavior.

That's what I was interested in studying in these rat moms without offspring (a model for stillbirth). I also compared their anxiety and depressive-like behavior to moms with offspring, non-moms, and non-moms exposed to offspring.

I found that "grieving mothers"—the mother rats that had their offspring permanently removed shortly after birth—showed increased depressive-like behavior, but not anxiety, weeks after giving birth, compared to the other female rats in the study (moms and non-moms). This finding was impressive for a couple of reasons. First, it showed that in animals, the breaking of the mother-infant bond can result in depressive-like behavior. Second, this effect is evident weeks later. And finally, it's not just pregnancy that is important for behavioral outcomes and brain changes with motherhood.

After these studies related to stillbirth and maternal mental health, there has been a bit of related research here and there, but nothing focused on pregnancy loss and the maternal brain.

Luckily, in 2020, this topic came up while talking to a friend and fellow researcher, Prof. Dr. Oliver Bosch, at the University of Regensburg, Germany. He has done fascinating research[269] on how partner loss affects the maternal brain and behavior, using the pair-bonding rodent, the prairie vole. He is also interested in how infant loss affects that maternal brain.

With Oliver and his doctoral student, Luisa Demarchi, we recently reviewed the impact of disrupting the mother-infant bond on the maternal brain. In this review[270], headed by Luisa, we highlight that neurons in the stress-reactivity system and the oxytocin system should be the focus of future research in this area. Both these systems are important for healthy mothering and the mother-infant bond, and both are activated with grief. Thus, when disrupted with pregnancy loss, it is likely that these two systems, and their actions within the brain, will be affected, having a cascade of effects throughout the maternal brain. As always, more research is needed, but overall it looks like the maternal brain is different if baby is not there. The brain functions differently, emotions are different. For example, if we extrapolate from offspring separation studies in rodents, repeated prolonged separation from offspring (typically three hours per day, or more) during the first week postpartum increases glucocorticoid receptor gene (Nr3C1) expression in the mothers' hippocampus[271], a gene linked to vulnerability and poor health outcomes. I suspect this has something to do with the fact that brain plasticity that started during pregnancy to prepare a female to mother is derailed with the loss of the infant. The mother-infant bond wasn't able to continue to form. The brain couldn't finish what it started.

## Moving forward

Sometimes, I think that one of the hardest parts of processing pregnancy loss must be the "taboo". Often miscarriages early in pregnancy are never talked about or there is a "you can try again" mentality. Women suffer in silence. Babies born dead also are not grieved. Often, there are no funerals and the mother must have weeks of physical reminders of her "failed" pregnancy. Maybe it's too heart breaking to talk about, maybe we just don't know what to say. However, we do know that you are meant to grieve. You must.

I'm from western Canada and spent nearly 11 years living in Vancouver. If you haven't been there you should go. It's a city on the Georgia Strait nestled into the North Shore Mountains. On ferry rides to Vancouver Island, further out on the Pacific Ocean, we would often see Orcas—those black whales with signature white markings. I actually had a roommate who studied the migration of these whales and learned that, even though they all look the same to me, they have distinct markings that can allow researchers, naturalists, and whale enthusiasts to follow individual animals for years. In 2018, an Orca mother, Tahlequah, caught international attention. For 17 days, she was seen carrying the body of her dead calf. It captured the world's attention and was an unprecedented event—never before had whale researchers "seen that kind of grief". In an article in *The Atlantic* titled *What A Grieving Orca Tells Us*[272], Ed Yong writes that "her grief has focused public attention in a way that conservationists hope will translate into political action." He quotes Ken Balcomb, of the Center for Whale Research: "She interpreted something to the world that I've been trying to adequately express to bureaucrats, politicians, and the public for 20 years: the need for salmon restoration" (which these orcas feed on almost exclusively and which is endangered due to human activities). The need for salmon restoration? What? That's the message she's telling us?

I think Tahlequah's story is more than that. For me, she expressed something to the world that we all need to see and accept: The emotional impact of pregnancy loss. The grief that goes with the breaking of a mother-infant bond. The need to grieve. It exists. Whether it's due to the physiological, psychological or neurobiological effects. The pain of pregnancy loss is real, even animals experience it.

Knowing how to grieve, how to sit with someone who is grieving, and how to move on is not easy. To my knowledge, there is no magic formula, but it is important to find a way that works for you. It is also important that our deceased children are never forgotten.

Talking about it can help. Either with a friend, with others who have experienced loss, or with a therapist. Having support is helpful. Grieving takes time. When I was a postdoctoral fellow, a friend at the time gave birth to a baby at 32 weeks gestation, due to unexpected pregnancy complications. The baby, as expected, lived for only a few minutes. She was able to share those minutes with her two older children and husband. It was a tragic event on many levels but the memories of that pregnancy and birth were not hidden, she shared them with friends and family. Shortly after her daughter's birth, she wrote on her Facebook page: "An angel in the book of life wrote down my baby's birth. And whispered as she closed the book 'too beautiful for earth'".

Chapter 21.

# Beyond "daddy blues"

I generally have focused my research on mothers for a number of reasons, primarily because I think that maternal perinatal mental illness has only recently been getting the attention that it deserves. I would like the focus to remain on mothers. But, am I being fair? Probably not. Anyone who struggles with a mental illness, especially a parent, deserves support and to feel well.

Over the past five years, it seems that there has been much more interest in how a father's mental health impacts offspring development, maternal mental health and the family in general.

In the media, talk about fathers struggling with mental illness is not as common as with mothers. It is much more difficult to find a famous father describing his struggles with perinatal depression than it is to find a famous mother living with perinatal depression. Fortunately, there are fathers talking about their struggles with mental illness and breaking the stigma of being "strong and silent" and becoming "brave and open" (a phrase I've stolen from author Elizabeth Lesser in *Cassandra Speaks*[273]).

"I thought being a dad for the first time was just going to be amazing. It wasn't what I expected at all. It was like I was holding someone else's baby...I just felt like I was failing, as a husband and as a father." says Tony in *Postnatal Depression in Men—BBC Stories*[274]. Brad explains that becoming a father "was the trigger for something in my mind to just go... boom".

In 2017, the television show *La Maison des Maternelles*, on France 5, had an episode dedicated to daddy blues[275] and invited a psychiatrist to speak about it. Fathers also shared their experiences on the episode.

Cyril, a new father, explained that he had "settled into a spiral, a vicious circle of negative emotions", and had experienced "guilt fed by a complete sense of incompetence". Bravo to this show for highlighting the fact that dads can struggle with a perinatal mental illness. Often, these illnesses are not as trivial as "daddy blues" but, in fact, can significantly impact a father's mental health.

## Sad dads or furious fathers?

In July of 2021, an article in the *New York Times* titled "I Gave Birth, but My Husband Developed Postpartum Depression[276]" helped to raise awareness of this phenomenon. The author of the article, Kim Hooper, who had a history of depression, writes: "I'd never thought about the possibility of men struggling with depression after the birth of a child. At the time I was focused on the well-being of our daughter, as well as my own physical and mental health. But men do struggle also."

A recent meta-analysis on the prevalence of prenatal and postpartum depression in fathers reports that 9.76% of fathers struggle with prenatal depression and 8.75% of fathers have postpartum depression (or depression in the first year after birth). That means nearly 1 in every 10 fathers struggles with depression. This is significant. Research has also noted that fathers' depressive symptoms peak between 3-6 months postpartum[277] and, rather than feelings of sadness, men may be more irritable, aggressive, and hostile. Fathers with depression, pre- or postnatally, may also use more drugs and alcohol, spend more time alone, and be distracted more easily.

Depression of one parent also has an impact on the other parent. Research shows that if one parent has depression there is a 24-50%[278] chance that the other parent will have depression. This is a high risk! Imagine the difficulty of trying to care for a newborn when neither parent is feeling well.

We also know that fathers, like mothers, have scary thoughts related to infant harm. In a recent study led by Dr. Nicole Fairbrother[279], whom I introduced in the chapter on perinatal anxiety, researchers looked at the rates of unwanted, intrusive thoughts in mothers and fathers in response to listening to a 10-minute audio recording of an infant crying. They found that 44% of parents in the postpartum period reported intrusive infant-related harm thoughts after they heard an infant cry. The researchers also found that there was no difference in the number of thoughts reported by mothers and fathers. Remember these are just thoughts and don't mean you have a mental illness. We all have thoughts that are unwanted. What's important to note here is that these types of thoughts are common and occur at the same rate in both mothers and fathers.

But what about anxiety disorders in fathers? A recent meta-analysis review[280] of the literature, using data from over 40,000 participants in 23 independent studies, found that 10.69% of dads will have an anxiety disorder during the perinatal period. Again 1 in 10 fathers will suffer, as with depression.

I also want to note here that I'm talking about fathers as they are the most studied partner in a parenting relationship because research on parenting is focused on heteronormative frameworks. However, we are starting to see a greater increase in research on LGBTQ+ parents and mental illness. We will have to wait for the results of these studies but, overall, I suspect that what we see in fathers in terms of mental illness would be what we see in any parenting partner.

## It takes two (to make a baby)

In a couple, it is often the mother who bears the "blame" for how a child will develop. There certainly is a large body of research (I can't tell you the exact number) showing the impact of a mother's stress or mental illness on offspring outcomes, in humans and animal models. There is no denying that there is an impact of early life stressors on child development, but these are not always related to the mother, and mothers are often a buffer against negative developmental outcomes.

Recent research[281] shows that a father's mental illness and stress can also impact child development. There are starting to be many interesting studies on this topic, which is beyond my expertise, but there is one study I wanted to point out here. As you may know, a large part of my research is based on how antidepressant medication use during the perinatal period affects mother and offspring[282]. For this research, I usually use animal models, in particular the Sprague-Dawley rat, a uniparental species (only the mother is the parent). So, I don't study dads. I also want to mention here that my research, and the clinical research available on this topic, points to the importance of effectively treating maternal mental illnesses, be that with antidepressant medications and/or other forms of treatment. This is the best option for both the mother and child.

I've also been curious about how a dad's antidepressant medication use affects the developing child. It's a question that isn't studied much because there isn't a direct link to the child; fathers aren't pregnant. But then again, they do provide the sperm and they are part of the home environment (at least in many households). In 2019, I attended and spoke at the *International Association of Women's Mental Health* conference[283]. After a talk on medication use during pregnancy and its impact on off-spring outcomes by another speaker, I raised my hand and asked, "what about a father's medication use and its impact on the offspring?". Clearly, the speaker hadn't thought about this. She gave me a funny look and dismissed the question. I'm guessing she had forgotten how a baby is made: an egg and a sperm.

In 2021, an article came out justifying my question (and pointing to my brilliance). The study[284], which was led by an international team of researchers, investigated the long-term effect of prenatal antidepressant use on the risk of mental health struggles in teenagers, using population-based health linked data. The researchers were able to access basic medical information from thousands of people in the medical system of the country they were doing their research in, Denmark (all research was ethically approved): diagnoses of mental illness, prescriptions, and birth data. They didn't have details of specific mood or anxiety symptoms so more research is needed in this area. What I found interesting about this research is that the impact of prenatal antidepressant use by both mothers and fathers on offspring outcomes was investigated. To my knowledge this is the first study of its kind.

This study showed that "children whose mothers continued antidepressants during pregnancy, had an increased risk of affective disorders, compared with children whose mothers discontinued before pregnancy. Similarly, continued paternal antidepressant use during pregnancy was associated with higher risk for offspring affective disorders, compared to discontinuation..." That means that antidepressant use during pregnancy in both mothers and fathers can impact mental health of teenagers.

Before you think that perinatal exposure to medications is not safe, reflect on this for a couple of minutes: First, if a fathers' medication use during pregnancy is related to a teenager's mental health then it's not the direct effect of the medication from the mother to the developing child that is a problem (crossing the placenta). In other words, mothers shouldn't feel guilty about taking their meds during pregnancy. Second, the authors point out that, although they investigated antidepressant medication effects, what this really indicates is that the severity of the underlying mental illness of each parent is having an impact on child development, not the medications. The authors go on to speculate that it is likely genetic and/or environmental factors that are important key components playing a role here.

I'll admit this isn't great news overall, because it points to the impact of a parent's mental health on offspring outcomes. But what it means to me is that the mental health of each parent is important, not just for them, but for their child as well. Perinatal mental health of fathers plays a significant role in a child's life. It's not just the mother who matters. We need to change the narrative around perinatal mental illness to bring awareness to the importance of mental health in all parents.

## Blame the brain

There are a number of factors that may be contributing to paternal perinatal depression including feeling trapped, the stress of financial responsibility, missing a sexual relationship, sleep deprivation, and a poor social network, to name a few. Biologically, we don't know much about perinatal depression in fathers but there is some research showing a relationship to brain changes.

In 2015, Dr. Pilyoung Kim and Dr. James Swain, then at Yale University, recruited 16 biological fathers of full-term and healthy infants to participate in a brain imaging study investigating how a father's depressive symptoms may be related to the father's brain grey matter volumes early in the postpartum period (2-4 weeks postpartum) and three months later (12-16 weeks postpartum[285]). Father's depressive symptoms were assessed by a standardized questionnaire and paternal sensitivity was assessed during a 5-minute parent-infant interaction.

When looking at the brain and behavior data, the researchers reported that lower levels of depressive symptoms, particularly those related to physical symptoms such as sleep and fatigue, were related to a greater increase in grey matter volume at 12-16 weeks postpartum in brain areas important for parental motivation such as the striatum, amygdala, and subgenual cortex. They also found that decreases in the grey matter volume of the orbitofrontal cortex (a brain area associated with decision making and related to parenting stress) was associated with higher levels of intrusiveness (for example, particularly physical manipulation of the infant's body) during father-infant interactions. The authors conclude that there are specific brain areas affected by depressive symptoms and related to early father-infant attachment. However, there is much more research to be done to understand the distinct change in the paternal brain of fathers at risk of developing perinatal depression or anxiety.

## Is it hormonal?

Apart from these neurobiological changes, hormones such as testosterone, cortisol, estrogens, vasopressin, oxytocin and prolactin have been speculated to play a role in paternal depression, because of their role in fatherhood. A few of these hormones have received significant scientific attention specifically in relation to paternal depression.

Testosterone, perhaps, has received the most recent attention. Research from Prof. Darby Saxbe's laboratory[286], at the University of Southern California, shows that high levels of testosterone in fathers may be protective against paternal postpartum depression, but be a risk to mothers and children. This seems like a bit of an odd finding so let's look briefly at the data. One hundred and forty-nine couples (fathers and mothers) participated in this study. Their testosterone levels were measured from saliva nine months after their infant was born. Different factors were evaluated in the mothers and fathers with the aid of standardized questionnaires: depressive symptoms, relationship satisfaction, parenting stress and intimate partner violence. Main findings from the study show that fathers' testosterone levels were associated with both maternal and paternal postpartum depressive symptoms, but in opposite directions. Fathers with lower testosterone at nine months postpartum reported more depressive symptoms, but their partners reported fewer depressive symptoms. On the other hand, higher paternal testosterone levels predicted adverse family outcomes, especially related to stress and intimate partner aggression at 15 months postpartum. These results are interesting and maybe a bit confusing, but the bottom line is that a father's testosterone levels play an important role in paternal postpartum depression, but also contribute to maternal depression and are related to stress and aggression in fathers. In order to improve mental health, parenting and child development, it is important to have a greater understanding of the dynamic changes in the postpartum period in relation to paternal and maternal depression.

Few fathers seek help for their mental illness. A recent study[287] of 1,989 fathers shows that only 3.2% of fathers sought mental health counselling in the past year, and as depressive symptoms increased in the fathers, they were less likely to seek help. We have yet to determine why this is the case, but likely the stigma of having a mental illness plays a significant role.

Kim Hooper (author of the *New York Times* article "I Gave Birth, but My Husband Developed Postpartum Depression" that I mentioned at the beginning of the chapter) wrote: "While maternal postpartum depression is widely discussed and recognized as a serious health issue, it's often hard for people to take seriously the idea of a man having similar problems. My husband, for one, found it ridiculous." Ironically, her husband ended up being the one diagnosed with postpartum depression.

Conclusion

# Maximizing mommy brain

To be honest my brain has not been 100% these past couple of weeks. The forgetfulness quotient is at a high. I'm not sure if this is related to having too many things on my mind, not sleeping as much as usual, or waking up last night to my son being sick with a stomach flu (why are they always starting at night!).

For me, forgetfulness or brain fog is a sign to step back and see how to take care of our brains. Easier said than done, and this likely could be a whole other book....but here are some key thoughts to maximize our mom brains.

## S.E.L.F.

Karen Kleiman wrote in her book, *The Art of Holding in Therapy*[288], about the notion of getting back to basics or what she calls S.E.L.F. These four letters stand for the following life basics that are important for us all and important for brain health, too.

### S – sleep.

Are you getting enough sleep? Can you sleep a bit more?

### E – exercise (movement).

Did you go for a walk today? Have you been moving enough?

**L – Laughter (or enjoyment).**

When was the last time you did something for you or something with your friends?

**F—Food (nutrition).**

How is your eating? Have you eaten anything fresh and colorful (naturally) lately?

There is also a growing body of literature focusing on different aspects of these four factors and parental brain health. Of course, there are many things that can help to optimize brain health, but as parents, we never have time to do them all. That's why it's best to take small steps: make one small, easy change for a week or two and then see if something else is needed. If we can improve even one of these aspects, it can be helpful in the long run.

## Support

Sometimes changing your routine or taking care of your S.E.L.F. is not enough, or is not possible. In these cases, interventions and treatments can help our brain health. These include things like parenting classes, group therapies, talk therapies, and medication. All of these can be beneficial for our parental brain and, although we don't yet know how these interventions alter a mother's brain circuitry (even medications[289]), we do know that they can be safe and effective treatment options.

One of my favorite interventions, which has recently been investigated by Dr. James Swain and colleagues[290] for its effects on the maternal brain, is *Mom Power* (an appropriate name). *Mom Power* is a program that supports families who are facing adversity and stress through the challenges of caring for young children, offering a strengths-based, nurturing approach to promoting resilience in parents and children.[291] This program provides families with training and in-session practice on positive parenting, child developmental needs, self-reflection, and perspective-taking. It was developed by the team of Dr. Maria Muzik, a psychiatrist at the University of Michigan. From what I understand, it is essentially a bringing together of mothers and children over a meal, one night per week for 13 weeks. There is also a similar therapy for dads, foster parents, childcare providers and military families.

Research on this program shows that mothers who participate in the program have reduced parenting stress, improved mental health (less depression and anxiety), and increased bonding and emotional responsiveness toward their children.[292] When we look at the brain, we also see changes.

In a study led by Dr. James Swain, maternal brain responses to child signals were studied in mothers that either participated in 10 weeks of *Mom Power* (14 mothers) or had 10 weeks of *Mom Power* curriculum content mailed to them (15 mothers)[293]. The brains of all the moms were scanned prior to and after 10 weeks of the intervention. Depression and parenting stress were also assessed by questionnaires. Brain scans were performed with fMRI to investigate functional responses to their own baby's cry, to another baby's cry, or to noise.

The results of the study show that participation in the *Mom Power* program reduced parenting stress and increased brain responses to child cues in social brain areas, such as the precuneus, and its functional connectivity with subgenual anterior cingulate cortex and amygdala; key components of neurocircuitry involved in self-awareness, decision-making, and emotional regulation. Thus, *Mom Power* improves brain function and connectivity in response to child distress. This is the first neuroimaging study to demonstrate that parental brain circuits for maternal care can be modulated by a type of therapy. This is quite remarkable.

Dr. Maria Muzik is also a remarkable clinician and scientist. We've chatted at conferences over the years. When I saw her give a keynote address at the 8th International Association for Women's Mental Health (IAWMH) meeting, in 2019, I was not only amazed by her *Mom Power* program, but I also loved the fact that, as a psychiatrist, Maria's goal is to not be needed. By developing programs like *Mom Power*, she is doing just that.

## It's your journey

Often, the advice given to new mothers revolves around the same themes: taking care of yourself, gaining confidence in what you are doing as a parent, and sharing responsibilities (if possible). A while back, I read these five tips on the Instagram account "Postpartum ta mere"[294]. I think they are quite fitting.

1. It's not a performance. Postpartum is a time of transition, there is no shame in living it badly and there is no trophy if you live it well. It is a stage to be lived as we can with our circumstances.

2. Express all your feelings and needs, even those that we don't understand or that we may be ashamed of (dare to say that we don't need to be with our baby for a while, etc.).

3. Make yourself a priority. You don't have to sacrifice yourself. Put the life jacket on yourself first, before you put it on your child.

4. Team up with the second parent (if there is one). There is no such thing as a primary parent and a secondary parent.

5. Do not idealize the lives of other parents.

And I would add that we need to remember that "Comparison is the thief of joy" (Theodore Roosevelt).

It can be challenging to navigate motherhood given the information that we are bombarded with through social media and society, in general. It is impossible to be a *good* mother by these standards. Dr. Sophie Brock[295] posts extensively about the social narrative of motherhood. In particular, she has written that "the social narrative of idealized Motherhood and the perfect mother myth leaves out our humanness, the messiness and complexity of us, our families, and our children. When we use these narratives as tools of measurement for how we're doing, and a compass for where we want to go—we'll end up lost, and think that it's our fault for not following the directions....our worthiness is inherent and not earned through our Motherhood. Our children want and need the best of who WE can be, not projections of a myth."

There are many right ways to mother and parent. Don't do what you should, do what works for you.

## Be natural

Part of this social narrative of the perfect mother myth often includes the idea of being "natural": giving birth naturally, feeding naturally, doing what nature intended as a mother. In truth, this word, "natural", encompasses many different realities. What is natural then, you ask? Let's look at the nature around us. There are the mother birds called Cuckoos that lay their eggs in another bird species' nest so that their offspring can be raised by other parents[296] (they don't parent at all). There are mammals, the naked mole rats, that have a queen who gives birth to all the offspring in the colony; the other females in the colony, who never reproduce, do most of the offspring care. There are animals, such as California mice, where both parents care in equal amounts for their young, and other animals where dads do the majority of the care. There are also insects and spider mothers who literally die caring for their young and are eaten by them (Imagine! Although I think sometimes we human moms nearly feel this will happen). There are also mothers who eat their offspring in times of threat, or let their offspring die because they don't have enough food, and so on. That is all "natural". Yes, all of it. "Natural" is more diverse than what we think.

## And of course...your brain is your superpower!

On Friday nights we have family movie nights at home, and last Friday we watched *The Incredibles 2*. You know, that animated film about a family of superheroes. The superhero dad takes care of the kids while his superhero wife is saving the world. Mr. Incredible, the dad, is overwhelmed by his son Jack-Jack's superpowers, so he goes to the home of the superhero costume designer, Edna Mode, to ask her for help. At one point, Edna Mode turns to him and says, "Parenting is a heroic task". Yes, Edna, parenting is a heroic task, and your parental brain is your superpower.

# Acknowledgements

I want to highlight that this book was the result of perseverance, patience and support from many. It has been a pleasure to work with Alix on the original French manuscript and it is because of her that this book exists.

I am thankful to my friends and colleagues who have contributed to this journey, for the support of the Institut des Neurosciences Cliniques de Rennes (www.incr.fr) for my research, and to my fellow researchers who publish on this topic—now more than ever. I'm also inspired by so many who work to ensure that mothers get the care and respect that they deserve. Thank you.

This book wouldn't be possible without the support of my parents and family. I am a parent, but I also still need mine.

To Thierry, my partner-in-parenting, my sweetie pie, who read this entire book more than once and provided important edits, thank you for doing life with me.

Finally, to my kids Zoé and Adam—thank you for letting me experience, firsthand, what I talk about. I love you.

# Endnotes

1   J. L. Pawluski, J. S. Lonstein, A. S. Fleming, The neurobiology of postpartum anxiety and depression, *Trends in Neurosciences*, 40(2):106-120, 2017.

2   www.jodipawluski.com/mommybrainrevisited

3   M. Numan *The Parental Brain*. Oxford University Press, 2020.

4   https://ninoute.wordpress.com

5   https://naitreetgrandir.com/blogue/2016/04/21/ou-est-passemon-cerveau

6   At the time of writing, her second child, a baby girl, was only a few months old.

7   A. Dowling, "Anne Hathaway's mommy brain struggle is real", *The Loop*, 29 July 2019.

8   A. Jarrahi-Zadeh, F. J. Kane, R. L. Van de Castle, P. A. Lachenbruch, K. A. Ewing, Emotional and cognitive changes in pregnancy and early puerperium, *The British Journal of Psychiatry*, 1969.

9   C. M. Poser, M. R. Kassirer, K. M. Peyser, Benign encephalopathy of pregnancy: Preliminary clinical observations, *Acta Neurologica Scandinavica*, 1986.

10  C. Parsons, S. Redman, Self-reported cognitive change during pregnancy, *The Australian Journal of Advanced Nursing*, 1991.

11  "What percentage of the US public approves of working wives?" *Our World in Data*. Retrieved 5 March 2020.

12  E. Badinter *The Conflict: How Modern Motherhood Undermines the Status of Women*. Metropolitan Books, 2012.

13  C. Delucena Meigs. *Females and Their diseases. A series of letters to his class*. Lea and Blanchard, 1848.

14  S. De Beauvoir. *Le Deuxième Sexe*, Gallimard, 1949.

15  Extract from *Sur la natalité*, a manuscript written in 1875 and cited in *Mother Nature* by Dr Sarah Blaffer Hrdy.

16  A. J. C. Cuddy, S. T. Fiske, P. Glick, When professionals become mothers, warmth doesn't cut the ice, *Journal of Social Issues*, 2004.

17  M. Hebl, E. B. King, P. Glick, S. L. Singletary, Hostile and benevolent reactions toward pregnant women: complementary interpersonal punishments and rewards that maintain traditional roles, *Journal of Applied Psychology*, 2007.

18  A. Malaika Tubbs. *The Three Mothers: How the Mothers of Martin Luther King, Jr., Malcolm X, and James Baldwin Shaped a Nation*. William Collins, 2021.

19   www.mothermag.com/anna-malaika-tubbs-the-three-mothers

20   www.inserm.fr/dossier/memoire

21   P. M. Brindle, M. W. Brown, J. Brown, H. B. Griffith, G. M. Turner, Objective and subjective memory impairment in pregnancy, *Psychological Medicine*, 1991.

22   A. Eidelman, N. W. Hoffmann, M. Kaitz, Cognitive deficits in women after childbirth, *Obstetrics and Gynecology*, 1993.

23   P. Casey, A longitudinal study of cognitive performance during pregnancy and new mother-hood, *Archives of Women's Mental Health*, 2000.

24   Henry JD, Rendell PG. A review of the impact of pregnancy on memory function. J Clin Exp Neuropsychol. 2007 Nov; 29(8):793-803.

25   H. Christensen et al., Cognition in pregnancy and motherhood: prospective cohort study, *The British Journal of Psychiatry*, 2010.

26   C. Cuttler, P. Graf, J. L. Pawluski, L. A. Galea, Everyday life memory deficits in pregnant women, *Canadian Journal of Experimental Psychology*, 2018.

27   L. A. Galea *et al.*, Spatial working memory and hippocampal size across pregnancy in rats, *Hormones and Behavior*, 2000.

28   Pawluski JL, Galea LA. Reproductive experience alters hippocampal neurogenesis during the postpartum period in the dam. Neuroscience. 2007 Oct 12;149(1):53-67; Pawluski JL, Walker SK, Galea LA. Reproductive experience differentially affects spatial reference and working memory performance in the mother. Horm Behav. 2006 Feb;49(2):143-9.

29   E. Hoekzema *et al.*, Pregnancy leads to long-lasting changes in human brain structure, *Nature Neuroscience*, 2016.

30   Laboratorio de Imagen Medica, Seccion Neuroimagen, Instituto de Investigacion Sanitaria Gregorio Maranon, Madrid, Espana.

31   www.jodipawluski.com/mommybrainrevisitedepisode/3f33e043/13-pregnancy -and-the-brain

32   M. A. Guevara et al., Verbal and visuospatial working memory during pregnancy: EEG correlation between the prefrontal and parietal cortices, *Neurobiology of Learning and Memory*, 2017.

33   J. G. Buckwalter et al., Pregnancy, the postpartum, and steroid hormones: effects on cognition and mood, *Psychoneuroendocrinology*, 1999.

34   J. F. Henry, B. B. Sherwin, Hormones and cognitive functioning during late pregnancy and postpartum: a longitudinal study, *Behavioural Neurosciences*, 2012.

35   Bardi M, Eckles M, Kirk E, Landis T, Evans S, Lambert KG. Parity modifies endocrine hormones in urine and problem-solving strategies of captive owl monkeys (Aotus spp.). Comp Med., 2014.

36   J. L. Pawluski, T. D. Charlier, S. E. Lieblich, G. L. Hammond, L. A. Galea, Reproductive experience alters corticosterone and CBG levels in the rat dam, *Physiology & Behavior*, 2009 and J. L. Pawluski, S. K. Walker, L. A. Galea, Reproductive experience differentially affects spatial reference and working memory performance in the mother, *Hormones and Behavior*, 2006.

37   C. Albin-Brooks, C. Nealer, S. Sabihi, A. Haim, B. Leuner, The influence of offspring, parity, and oxytocin on cognitive flexibility during the postpartum period, *Hormones and Behavior*, 2017.

38   C. M. Vanston, N. V. Watson, Selective and persistent effect of foetal sex on

cognition in pregnant women, *NeuroReport*, 2005.

39    A. Swain *et al.*, A prospective study of sleep, mood, and cognitive function in postpartum and nonpostpartum women, *Sleep patterns*, 1997.

40    H. J. V. Rutherford *et al.*, Maternal working memory, emotion regulation, and responsivity to infant distress, *Journal of Applied Developmental Psychology*, 2020.

41    Episode 25. Brain Activity from Pregnancy to Postpartum. *Mommy Brain Revisited* Podcast.

42    A. J. Groner *et al.*, A randomized trial of oral iron on tests of short-term memory and attention span in young pregnant women, *Journal of Adolescent Health Care*, 1986.

43    V. A. Purvin, D. W. Dunn, Caffeine and the benign encephalopathy of pregnancy, *Acta Neurologica Scandinavica*, 1987.

44    M. Casertano, V. Fogliano, D. Ercolini, Psychobiotics, gut microbiota and fermented foods can help preserve mental health, *Food Research International*, 2022.

45    M. Brett, S. Baxendale, Motherhood and memory: a review, *Psychoneuroendocrinology*, 2001.

46    B. Harris et al., Cardiff puerperal mood and hormone study. III. Postnatal depression at 5 to 6 weeks postpartum, and its hormonal correlates across the peripartum period, *The British Journal of Psychiatry*, 1996.

47    R. A. Crawley et al., Cognition in pregnancy and the first year post-partum, *Psychology and Psychotherapy*, 2003.

48    S. J. Davies et al., Cognitive impairment during pregnancy: a meta-analysis, *The Medical Journal of Australia*, 2018.

49    www.jodipawluski.com/mommybrainrevisited/episode/dfbc7b52/5-mommy-brain-during -pregnancywhat-does-the-science-say

50    L. A. Galea *et al.*, Spatial working memory and hippocampal size across pregnancy in rats, art. cit.

51    M. Darnaudery *et al.*, Early motherhood in rats is associated with a modification of hippocampal function, *Psychoneuroendocrinology*, 2007.

52    C. H. Kinsley *et al.*, Motherhood improves learning and memory, *Nature*, 1999.

53    https://qz.com/590486/scientists-think-baby-brain-makes-yousmarter-and-more-organized -not-less

54    J. L. Pawluski, Neuroplasticity in the maternal hippocampus: Relation to cognition and effects of repeated stress, *Hormones and Behavior*, 2016.

55    J. L. Pawluski, S. K. Walker, L. A. Galea, Reproductive experience differentially affects spatial reference and working memory performance in the mother, art. cit. J. L. Pawluski, B. L. Vanderbyl, K. Ragan, L. A. Galea, First reproductive experience persistently affects spatial reference and working memory in the mother and these effects are not due to pregnancy or "mothering" alone, *Behavioural Brain Research*, 2006.

56    J. G. Buckwalter et al., Pregnancy, the postpartum, and steroid hormones: effects on cognition and mood, *Psychoneuroendocrinology*, 1999.

57    J. G. Buckwalter et al., Pregnancy and postpartum: changes in cognition and mood, *Progress in Brain Research*, 2001.

58    V. Miller, L. A. VanWormer, A. Veile, Assessment of attention in biological

mothers using the attention network test, *Current Psychology,* 2020.

59  www.jodipawluski.com/mommybrainrevisited/episode/2fbdc63d/9-post partum-attention-an -important-component-of-mommybrain

60  J. L. Pawluski, K. G. Lambert, C. H. Kinsley, Neuroplasticity in the maternal hippocampus: Relation to cognition and effects of repeated stress, *Hormones and Behavior,* 2016.

61  B. Leuner *et al.,* The influence of offspring, parity, and oxytocin on cognitive flexibility during the postpartum period, *Hormones and Behavior,* 2017. /V. Lemaire *et al.,* Motherhood-induced memory improvement persists across lifespan in rats but is abolished by a gestational stress, *European Journal of Neuroscience,* 2006.

62  K. Ning *et al.,* Parity is associated with cognitive function and brain age in both females and males, *Scientific Reports,* 2020.

63  E. R. Orchard *et al.,* Relationship between parenthood and cortical thickness in late adulthood, *PLoS ONE,* 2020.

64  https://www.todaysparent.com/family/parenting/baby-brain-is-bs

65  M. Kaitz *et al.,* Parturient women can recognize their infants by touch, *Developmental Psychology,* 1992. M. Kaitz *et al.,* Fathers can also recognize their newborns by touch, *Infant Behavior and Development,* 1994.

66  I. U. Yarube *et al.,* Cognitive dysfunction among primi gravidae attending an ante natal clinic in Kano, Northwest Nigeria, *Nigerian Journal of Physiological Sciences,* 2019.

67  In D. F. Sherry, E. Hampson, Evolution and the hormonal control of sexually-dimorphic spatial abilities in humans, *Trends in Cognitive Sciences,* 1997.

68  C. M. Jones, V. A. Braithwaite, S. D. Healy, The evolution of sex differences in spatial ability, *Behavioral Neuroscience,* 2003. D. F. Sherry, E. Hampson, Evolution and the hormonal control of sexually-dimorphic spatial abilities in humans, Trends in Cognitive Sciences, 1997.

69  M. V. Anderson, M. D. Rutherford, Evidence of a nesting psychology uring human pregnancy, *Evolution and Human Behavior,* 2013.

70  https://dictionary.apa.org/primary-maternal-preoccupation

71  B. Callaghan *et al.,* Evidence for cognitive plasticity during pregnancy via enhanced learning and memory, *Memory,* 2022.

72  C. McCormack, BL. Callaghan, JL. Pawluski. It's Time to Rebrand "Mommy Brain". *JAMA Neurology.* 2023 Apr 1;80(4):335-336.

73  J. P.J. Pinel, *Biopsychology,* 3rd edition. Pearson. 1996.

74  J. Balthazart. *Quand le cerveau devient masculin.* Humen Sciences Éditions, 2019.

75  K. M. Lenz, B. M. Nugent, M. M. McCarthy, Sexual differentiation of the rodent brain: dogma and beyond, *Frontiers in Neuroscience,* 2012.

76  D. Joel, Beyond the binary: Rethinking sex and the brain, *Neuroscience & Biobehavioral Reviews,* 2021.

77  *Ibid.* D. Joel, M. M. McCarthy, Incorporating sex as a biological variable in neuropsychiatric research: Where are we now and where should we be?, *Neuropsychopharmacology,* 2016.

78  J. L. Pawluski, N. Kokras, T. D. Charlier, C. Dalla, Sex matters in neuroscience and neuro-psychopharmacology, *European Journal of Neuroscience,* 2020.

79 National Institutes of Health : NIH, USA NOT-OD-15-102, Consideration of Sex as a Biological Variable in NIH-funded Research.

80 W. Leung, It's not like there's an instinct called mothering, theglobeandmail.com, 9 mai 2013.

81 https://www.oed.com/viewdictionaryentry/Entry/110566#:~:text=Thesaurus%20%C2%BB-,a.,Cf.

82 E. Badinter. *L'amour en plus*. Le Livre de Poche, 2001.

83 S. Blaffer Hrdy. *Mother Nature*. Ballantine Books, 2000.

84 A. Bartels, S. Zeki, The neural correlates of maternal and romantic love, *Neuro-Image*, 2004.

85 A. Bartels, S. Zeki, The neural basis of romantic love, *NeuroReport*, 2000.

86 R. Feldman, The adaptive human parental brain: implications for children's social development, *Trends in Neurosciences*, 2015.

87 M. Numan, *The Parental Brain*, Oxford University Press, 2020.

88 www.jodipawluski.com/mommybrainrevisited/episode/ 33lcd2c9/21-oxytocin -and-bonding

89 J. Wartella *et al.*, Single or multiple reproductive experiences attenuate neurobehavioral stress and fear responses in the female rat, *Physiology & Behavior*, 2003.

90 J. L. Pawluski, E. Hoekzema, J. S. Lonstein, B. Leuner, Less can be more: Fine tuning the maternal brain, *Neurosciences & Biobehavioral Reviews*, 2021.

91 A. Oatridge *et al.*, Change in brain size during and after pregnancy : study in healthy women and women with preeclampsia, *American Journal of Neuroradiology*, 2002.

92 E. Hoekzema *et al.*, Pregnancy leads to long-lasting changes in human brain structure, *Nat Neurosci.* 2017 Feb;20(2):287-296.

93 The grey matter of the brain contains the cell bodies of the neurons (the white matter contains the nerve fibers).

94 M. Martínez-García *et al.*, Do pregnancy-induced brain changes reverse? The brain of a mother six years after parturition, *Brain Sciences*, 2021.

95 The gyri are sets of sinuous folds on the surface of the brain. Each lobe is composed of a number of gyri.

96 White matter is the set of fibers that allow the different parts of our brain to be connected and to communicate with each other.

97 S. Zhang *et al.*, Aberrant resting-state interhemispheric functional onnectivity in patients with postpartum depression, *Behavioural Brain Research*, 2020.

98 P. Kim *et al.*, The plasticity of human maternal brain: Longitudinal changes in brain anatomy during the early postpar- tum period, *Behavioral Neuroscience*, 2010. N. Lisofsky et al., Postpartal neural plasticity of the maternal brain: Early renormalization of pregnancy-related decreases?, *Neuro-Signals*, 2019.

99 E. Luders *et al.*, From baby brain to mommy brain: Widespread gray matter gain after giving birth, *Cortex*, 2020.

100 The Society for Neuroscience in 2017, The International Association for Women's Mental Health in Paris in 2018 and more recently at the hybrid meeting of the International Behavioral Neuroscience Society meeting in 2021.

101 https://www.jodipawluski.com/mommybrainrevisited/episode/3f33e043/13
-pregnancy-and-the-brain

102 J. L. Pawluski, L. A. Galea, Reproductive experience alters hippocampal neurogenesis during the postpartum period in the dam, *Neuroscience*, 2007.

103 J. L. Pawluski, K. G. Lambert, C. H. Kinsley, Neuroplasticity in the maternal hippocampus: Relation to cognition and effects of repeated stress, *Hormones and Behavior*, 2016.

104 J. L. Pawluski *et al.*, Effect of sertraline on central serotonin and hippocampal plasticity in pregnant and non-pregnant rats, *Neuropharmacology*, 2020.

105 A. Haim et al 2017. A survey of neuroimmune changes in pregnant and post-partum female rats, *Brain Behav Immun*, 2017.

106 https://www.jodipawluski.com/mommybrainrevisited/episode/ca788b08/16
-immune-changes-in-the-maternal-brain

107 National Research Institute for Agriculture, Food and the Environment (in french, the acronyme stands for: Institut national de recherche pour l'agriculture, l'alimentation et l'environnement).

108 M. Brus, M. Meurisse, M. Keller, F. Lévy. Interactions with the young down-regulate adult olfactory neurogenesis and enhance the maturation of olfactory neuroblasts in sheep mothers. Front Behav Neurosci. 2014.

109 T. Shingo *et al.*, Pregnancy-stimulated neurogenesis in the adult female forebrain mediated by prolactin, *Science*, 2003.

110 C. A. Penick *et al.*, Reversible plasticity in brain size, behaviour and physiology characterizes caste transitions in a socially flexible ant (*Harpegnathos saltator*), *Proceeding of The Royal Society B. Biological Sciences*, 2021.

111 For more see J. L. Pawluski *et al.*, Less can be more: Fine tuning the maternal *Neuroscience and Biobehavioral Reviews,* 2022.

112 D. A. Barrière *et al.*, Brain orchestration of pregnancy and maternal behavior in mice: A longitudinal morphometric study, *NeuroImage*, 2021.

113 www.sciencedirect.com/science/article/pii/S10538 11921000537?via%3Dihub #sec0023

114 www.pbbmedia.org/matrescence.html

115 S. Carmona *et al.*, Pregnancy and adolescence entail similar neuroanatomical adaptations: A comparative analysis of cerebral morphometric changes, *Human Brain Mapping*, 2019.

116 Most of the references used in this chapter come from the following review article: J. L. Pawluski, E. Hoekzema, J. S. Lonstein, B. Leuner, "Less can be more: Fine tuning the maternal brain," *Neuroscience and Biobehavioral Reviews*, 2022.

117 J. P. Lorberbaum *et al.*, Feasibility of using fMRI to study mothers responding to infant cries, *Depression and Anxiety*, 1999.

118 S. Raz, Behavioral and neural correlates of cognitive-affective function during late pregnancy: An event-related potentials study, *Behavioural Brain Research*, 2014.

119 A. Roos *et al.*, Selective attention to fearful faces during pregnancy, *Progress in Neuro-Psychophar-macology & Biological Psychiatry*, 2012.

120 M. V. Anderson, M. D. Rutherford, Recognition of novel faces after single exposure is enhanced during pregnancy, *Evolutionary Psychology*, 2011.

121  R. M. Pearson *et al.*, Emotional sensitivity of motherhood: late pregnancy is associated with enhanced accuracy to encode emotional faces, *Hormones and Behavior*, 2009.

122  B. C. Jones *et al.*, Menstrual cycle, pregnancy and oral contraceptive use alter attraction to apparent health in faces, *Proceedings of the Royal Society B. Biological Sciences*, 2005.

123  H. J. V. Rutherford *et al.*, Prenatal neural responses to infant faces predict postpartum reflective functioning, *Infant Behavior & Development*, 2018.

124  J. Dudek *et al.*, Changes in cortical sensitivity to infant facial cues from pregnancy to motherhood predict mother-infant bon- ding, *Child Development*, 2020.

125  A. J. Bjertrup *et al.*, The maternal brain: Neural responses to infants in mothers with and without mood disorder, *Neuroscience & Biobehavioral Reviews*, 2019.

126  *Ibid.*

127  J. L. Pawluski *et al.*, Less can be more: Fine tuning the matenal brain, art. cit.

128  P. J. Brunton, J. A. Russell, The expectant brain: Adapting for motherhood, *Nature Reviews. Neuroscience*, 2008. M. Rincón-Cortés, A. A. Grace, Adaptations in reward-related behaviors and mesolimbic dopamine function during motherhood and the postpartum period, *Frontiers in Neuroendocrinology*, 2020.

129  S. Atzil *et al.*, Dopamine in the medial amygdala network mediates human bonding, *PNAS*, 2017.

130  R. C. Froemke, L. J. Young, Oxytocin, neural plasticity, and social behavior, *Annual Review of Neuroscience*, 2021.

131  J. L. Pawluski *et al.*, Less can be more: Fine tuning the maternal brain, *Neuroscience & Biobehavioral Reviews*, 2022.

132  E. Leibenluft *et al.*, Mothers' neural activation in response to pictures of their children and other children, *Biological Psychiatry*, 2004.

133  J. E. Swain *et al.*, Baby stimuli and the parent brain: functional neuroimaging of the neural substrates of parent-infant attachment, *Psychiatry (Edgmont)*, 2008.

134  H. K. Laurent, J. C. Ablow, The missing link: Mothers' neural response to infant cry related to infant attachment behaviors, *Infant Behavior & Development*, 2012.

135  E. D. Musser *et al.*, The neural correlates of maternal sensitivity: An fMRI study, *Developmental Cognitive Neuroscience*, 2012.

136  C. E. Parsons *et al.*, Duration of motherhood has incremental effects on mothers' neural processing of infant vocal cues: a neuroimaging study of women, *Scientific Reports*, 2017.

137  K. Zhang *et al.*, Dynamic alterations in spontaneous brain activity in mothers: A resting-state functional magnetic resonance imaging study, *Neuroscience Bulletin*, 2019.

138  A. J. Dufford *et al.*, Maternal brain resting-state connectivity in the postpartum period, *Journal of Neuroendocrinology*, 2019.

139  R. S. Bridges, Long-term effects of pregnancy and parturition upon maternal responsiveness in the rat, *Physiology & Behavior*, 1975. B. G. Orpen, A. S. Fleming, Experience with pups sustains maternal responding in postpartum rats, *Physiology & Behavior*, 1987.

140  M. Pérez-Hernández *et al.*, Multiparity decreases the effect of distractor stimuli on a working memory task: An EEG study, *Social Neuroscience*, 2021.

141  C. F. Boukydis, R. L. Burgess, Adult physiological response to infant cries: Effects of temperament of infant, parental status, and gender, *Child Development*, 1982.

142  J. L. Pawluski, L. A. Galea, Reproductive experience alters hippocampal neurogenesis during the postpartum period in the dam, *Neuroscience*, 2006.

143  A. N. Maupin *et al.*, Investigating the association between parity and the maternal neural response to infant cues, *Social Neuroscience*, 2018.

144  This chapter has been modified from a blog I wrote: www.inspirethemind.org/blog/mom-brain-forever

145  A.-M. G. de Lange *et al.*, Population-based neuroimaging reveals traces of childbirth in the maternal brain, *Proceedings of the National Academy of Sciences of the United States of America (PNAS)*, 2019.

146  E. Hoekzema *et al.*, Pregnancy leads to long-lasting changes in human brain structure, art. cit.

147  J. L. Pawluski *et al.*, Neuroplasticity in the maternal hippocampus: Relation to cognition and effects of repeated stress, *Hormones and Behavior*, 2016.

148  www.jodipawluski.com/mommybrainrevisited/episode/ 483f4c2e/27-motherhood -and-brain-aging

149  www.ukbiobank.ac.uk

150  A.-M. G. de Lange *et al.*, The maternal brain: Region-specific patterns of brain aging are traceable decades after childbirth, *Human Brain Mapping*, 2020.

151  I. Voldsbekk *et al.*, A history of previous childbirths is linked to women's white matter brain age in midlife and older age, *Human Brain Mapping*, 2021.

152  K. Ning *et al.*, Parity is associated with cognitive function and brain age in both females and males, art. cit.

153  E. R. Orchard *et al.*, Relationship between parenthood and cortical thickness in late adulthood, art. cit.

154  E. R. Orchard *et al.*, Neuroprotective effects of motherhood on brain function in late life: A resting-state fMRI study, *Cerebral Cortex*, 2021.

155  www.jodipawluski.com/mommybrainrevisited/episode/1e0d0c7f/15-enduring-effects-of -parenting-on-the-brain

156  www.youtube.com/watch?v=hfBjKOGlFkw

157  Source: The National Institute of Statistics and Economic Studies (INSEE) which is the national statistics bureau of France.

158  J. L. Pawluski, L. A. Galea, Reproductive experience alters hippocampal neurogenesis during the postpartum period in the dam, art. cit.

159  Pawluski JL, Galea LA. Reproductive experience alters hippocampal neurogenesis during the postpartum period in the dam. Neuroscience. 2007 Oct 12;149(1): 53-67.

160  C. Zhao, W. Deng, F. H. Gage, Mechanisms and functional implications of adult neurogenesis, *Cell*, 2008.

161  J. Bick *et al.*, Foster mother-infant bonding: associations between foster mothers' oxytocin production, electrophysiological brain activity, feelings of commitment, and caregiving quality, *Child Development*, 2013.

162  Behavioural happiness is a behavioural variable defined as a set of behaviours including positive affect, smiling, praise and active encouragement for mutual

interactions that are recognized as important when caring for a foster child. J. Bick, M. Dozier, K. Bernard, D. Grasso, R. Simons, "Foster mother-infant bonding: associations between foster mothers' oxytocin production, electrophysiological brain activity, feelings of commitment, and caregiving quality," art. cit.

163  M. Hernández-González et al., Observing videos of a baby crying or smiling induces similar, but not identical, electroencephalographic responses in biological and adoptive mothers, Infant Behavior & Development, 2016.

164  Pérez-Hernández M, Hernández-González M, Hidalgo-Aguirre RM, Amezcua-Gutiérrez C, Guevara MA. Listening to a baby crying induces higher electro-encephalographic synchronization among prefrontal, temporal and parietal cortices in adoptive mothers. Infant Behav Dev. 2017 May;47:1-12.

165  U. Henz, Fathers' involvement with their children in the United Kingdom: Recent trends and class differences, Demographic Research, 2019. X. Li, Fathers' involvement in Chinese societies: increasing presence, uneven progress, Child Development Perspectives, 2020.

166  E. Abraham, R. Feldman, The neurobiology of human allomaternal are; implications for fathering, coparenting, and children's social development, Physiology & Behavior, 2018.

167  Some of this section has been modified from M. Martínez-García, S. I. Cardenas, J. Pawluski, S. Carmona, D. E. Saxbe, "Recent Neuroscience Advances in Human Parenting," in G. González-Mariscal (ed.), Patterns of Parental Behavior, Springer, 2022.

168  P. Kim, Neural plasticity in fathers of human infants, Social Neuroscience, 2014.

169  P. Kim et al., The plasticity of human maternal brain: Longitudinal changes in brain anatomy during the early postpartum period, art. cit.

170  M. Martínez-García, S. I. Cardenas, J. Pawluski, S. Carmona, D. E. Saxbe, Recent Neuro-science Advances in Human Parenting, op. cit.

171  M. Paternina-Die et al., The paternal transition entails neuroanatomic daptations that are associated with the father's brain response to his infant cues, Cerebral Cortex Communications, 2020.

172  E. Hoekzema et al., Pregnancy leads to long-lasting changes in human brain structure, art. cit.

173  R. Feldman et al., The neural mechanisms and consequences of paternal caregiving, Nature Reviews. Neuroscience, 2019.

174  K. E. Wynne-Edwards, Hormonal changes in mammalian fathers, Hormones and Behavior, 2001.

175  F. Diaz-Rojas et al., Development of the paternal brain in expectant fathers during early pregnancy, NeuroImage, 2021.

176  J. K. Rilling et al., The neural correlates of paternal consoling behavior and frustration in response to infant crying, Developmental Psychobiology, 2021.

177  E. Abraham et al., Father's brain is sensitive to childcare experiences, PNAS, 2014.

178  www.jodipawluski.com/mommybrainrevisited/episode/4606760b/29-fatherhood-and -the-brain

179  J. K. Rilling, J. S. Mascaro, P. D. Hackett, Differential neural responses to child and sexual stimuli in human fathers and non-fathers and their hormonal correlates, Psychoneuroendocrinology, 2014.

180  M. A. Shir Atzil *et al.*, Synchrony and specificity in the maternal and the paternal brain: Relations to oxytocin and vasopressin, *Journal of the American Academy of Child & Adolescent Psychiatry*, 2012.

181  Z. Wu *et al.*, Galanin neurons in the medial preoptic area govern parental behaviour, *Nature*, 2014.

182  www.jodipawluski.com/mommybrainrevisited/episode/30lda5f7/19-the-neurons-essential-for-parenting

183  J. K. Rilling, A. Gonzalez, M. Lee, The neural correlates of grandmaternal caregiving, *Proceedings of the Royal Society B*, 2021.

184  L. Geddes. "Grandmothers may be more connected to grandchildren than to own offspring", *The Guardian*, 17 Novembre 2021.

185  https://edition.cnn.com/2021/11/19/health/grandparent-empathy-children-study-wellness/index.html

186  E. Abraham *et al.*, Father's brain is sensitive to childcare experiences, art. cit.

187  P. Kim, How stress can influence brain adaptations to motherhood, *Frontiers Neuroendocrinology*, 2021. My podcast with her: www.jodipawluski.com/mommybrainrevisited/episode/35d37e2f/17-stress-and-the-maternal-brain

188  K. L. D'Anna-Hernandez *et al.*, Acculturation, mater- nal cortisol, and birth outcomes in women of Mexican des cent, *Psychosomatic Medicine*, 2012. My podcast with her: www.jodipawluski.com/mommybrainrevisited/episode/33c6fdd2/26-sociocultural-stress-and-maternal-mental-health

189  This chapter is adapted from another chapter I wrote in *You are not alone: An anthology of perinatal mental health stories from conception to postpartum*, by the Canadian Perinatal Mental Health Collaborative, Wintertickle Press, 2021.

190  Clémentine Galey de Bliss Stories: Toutes les Bliss-girls sont des guerrières Hachette.fr, 24th august of 2020.

191  J. L. Pawluski, J. S. Lonstein, A. S. Fleming, "The neurobiology of postpartum anxiety and depression", *Trends in Neurosciences*, 40(2):106-120, 2017.

192  P. A. Coble, N. L. Day, The epidemiology of mental and emotional disorders during pregnancy and the postpartum period, in R. L. Cohen (dir.), *Psychiatric Consultation in Childbirth Settings*, Springer, 1998.

193  T. Munk-Olsen *et al.*, Perinatal psychiatric episodes: A population-based study on treatment incidence and prevalence, *Translational Psychiatry*, 2016.

194  https://www.jodipawluski.com/mommybrainrevisited/episode/ca788b08/16-immune-changes-in-the-maternal-brain

195  I. Brockington, A historical perspective on the psychiatry of motherhood, in A. Riecher-Rossler (dir.), *Perinatal Stress, Mood and Anxiety Disorders*, Karger, 2005.

196  J.-E. Esquirol, *Des maladies mentales considérées sous les rapports médical, hygiénique et médico-légal*. J.B. Bailliere, 1838.

197  K. Trede, R. J. Baldessarini, A. C. Viguera, A. Bottero, Treatise on insanity in pregnant, postpartum, and lactating women (1858) by Louis Victor Marcé: a commentary, *Harvard Review of Psychiatry*, 2009.

198  https://marcesociety.com

199  V. Sharma, A. Santopinto, Childbirth and manic-depressive illness: An account of Emil Kraepelin's contribution, *German Journal of Psychiatry*, 2008.

200  M. N. Marks, Introduction: Professor Channi Kumar (1938-2000), *The British Journal of Psychiatry*, Supplement, 2004.

201  https://www.today.com/popculture/brooke-shields-blasts-cruises-ridiculous-rant-wbna 8427947

202  *Diagnostic and Statistical Manual of Mental Disorders*, 5th edition, APA, 2013.

203  M.-N. Vacheron et al, "National Expert Committee on Maternal Mortality, Maternal Mortality by Suicide in France 2013-2015," *Gynecology Obstetrics Fertility & Senology*, 2021.

204  S. Grigoriadis et al., Perinatal suicide in Ontario, Canada: a 15-year population-based study, *Canadian Medical Association Journal*, 2017.

205  C. Billionnet *et al.*, Gestational diabetes and adverse perinatal out-comes from 716 152 births in France in 2012, *Diabetologia*, 2017.

206  World Health Organization, Mental health and substance use.

207  J. L. Pawluski, J. S. Lonstein, A. S. Fleming, "The neurobiology of postpartum anxiety and depression", *Trends in Neurosciences*, 40(2):106-120, 2017.

208  Translated as *Violence and Support in Motherhood*.

209  https://perinat2020.sciencesconf.org

210  https://pubmed.ncbi.nlm.nih.gov

211  K. E. Wonch, C. B. de Medeiros, J. A. Barrett, A. Dudin,W. A. Cunningham, G. B. Hall, M. Steiner, A. S. Fleming Postpartum depression and brain response to infants: Differential amygdala response and connectivity, *Social Neuroscience*, 2016.

212  J. L. Pawluski, J. S. Lonstein, A. S. Fleming, "The neurobiology of postpartum anxiety and depression", *Trends in Neurosciences*, 40(2):106-120, 2017.

213  A. Dudin *et al.*, Amygdala and affective responses to infant pictures: Comparing depressed and non-depressed mothers and non-mothers, *Journal of Neuro-endocrinology*, 2019. / Mommy Brain Revisited episode 22.

214  M. J. Dickens, J. L. Pawluski, The HPA axis during the peri- natal period : Implications for perinatal depression, *Endocrinology*, 2018. J. Pawluski, M. Dickens, J. Maguire, Neuroendocrinology of perinatal mental illness, *in* P. J. Brunton et D. R. Grattan (dir.), *Neuroendocrinology of Pregnancy and Lactation*, Springer Nature Switzerland AG (in print).

215  M. J. Dickens, J. L. Pawluski, The HPA axis during the perinatal period: Implications for perinatal depression, Endocrinology, 2018.

216  C. Conaboy. "Motherhood brings the most dramatic brain changes of a woman's life" *The Boston Globe*. July 17, 2018.

217  E. J. Unsworth. *After the Storm: Postnatal Depression and the Utter Weirdness of New Motherhood*. Wellcome Collection, Main Edition, 2021.

218  K. Kleiman. *Good moms have scary thoughts*. Familius, 2019.

219  https://www.etalk.ca/celebrity/alanis-morissette-gets-real-about-postpartum-activity.html

220  P. J. Lawrence, Intrusive thoughts and images of intentional harm to infants in the context of maternal postnatal depression, anxiety, and OCD, *British Journal of General Practice*, 2017.

221  K. R. Thorsness, C. Watson, E. M. LaRusso, Perinatal anxiety: approach to

diagnosis and management in the obstetric setting, *American Journal of Obstetrics and Gynecology*, 2018.

222 DSM-5 (*Manuel diagnostique et statistique des troubles mentaux*, 5e édition).

223 OCD is no longer considered an anxiety disorder in the DSM-5. It is in he category of "obsessive-compulsive and related disorders". In the ICD-10 (International Classification of Diseases, 10th Revision), it is still listed as an anxiety disorder (www.icd10data.com/ICD10CM/ Codes/F01-F99/F40-F48/F42-/F42.9).

224 E. J. Fawcett *et al.*, The prevalence of anxiety disorders during pregnancy and the postpartum period: A multivariate bayesian meta-analysis, *The Journal of Clinical Psychiatry*, 2020.

225 Source: American Psychiatric Association.

226 Source: National Institute of Mental Health.

227 C. Conaboy. "Motherhood brings the most dramatic brain changes of a woman's life" *The Boston Globe*. July 17, 2018.

228 J. H. Goodman, G. R. Watson, B. Stubbs, Anxiety disorders in postpartum women: A systematic review and meta-analysis, *Journal of Affective Disorders*, 2016.

229 https://podcasts.apple.com/fr/podcast/mommy-brain-revisited/id1512717675

230 J. L. Pawluski, J. E. Swain, J. S. Lonstein, Neurobiology of peripartum mental illness, *Handbook of Clinical Neurology*, 2021.

231 A. S. Fleming *et al.*, Maternal affect and quality of parenting experiences are related to amy-gdala response to infant faces, *Social Neuroscience*, 2012.

232 Measured with the blood oxygenation level-dependent signal (Bold).

233 K. E. Wonch *et al.*, Postpartum depression and brain response to infants: Differential amygdala response and connectivity, art. cit.

234 S. M. Malak *et al.*, Maternal anxiety and neural responses to infant faces, *Journal of Affective Disorders*, 2015.

235 J. Pawluski, M. Dickens, J. Maguire, "Neuroendocrinology of perinatal mental illness", *in* P. J. Brunton et D. R. Grattan (dir.), *Neuroendocrinology of Pregnancy and Lactation*. Springer Nature Switzerland AG (in print).

236 www.app-network.org

237 www.jodipawluski.com/mommybrainrevisited/episode/2df803c3/20-the-neuro biology-of-postpartum-psychosis

238 P. Dazzan *et al.*, Brain structure in women at risk of postpartum psychosis: an MRI study, *Translational Psychiatry*, 2017.

239 Women with previously diagnosed bipolar disorder.

240 P. Dazzan *et al.*, Neurocognitive correlates of working memory and emotional processing in postpartum psychosis: an fMRI study, *Psychological Medicine*, 2021.

241 https://afar.info

242 Translated as *Violence and Support in Motherhood*.

243 National confidential inquiry of maternal deaths (ENCMM), Inserm et Santé publique France, www. santepubliquefrance.fr/etudes-et-enquetes/enquete-nationale-confidentielle-sur-les -morts-maternelles

244 C.A. Stramrood *et al.* Posttraumatic stress disorder following preeclampsia and PPROM: a prospective study with 15 months follow-up, *Reproductive Sciences*, 2011.

245 S. Dekel *et al.*, Childbirth induced posttraumatic stress syndrome: A systematic review of prevalence and risk factors, *Frontiers in Psychology*, 2017.

246 E. Schobinger, S. Stuijfzand, A. Horsch, Acute and post- traumatic stress disorder symptoms in mothers and fathers following childbirth: A prospective cohort study, *Frontiers in Psychiatry*, 2020.

247 *Ibid.*

248 C. Deforges, Y. Noël, M. Eberhard-Gran, S. Garthus-Niegel, A. Horsch, Prenatal insomnia and childbirth-related PTSD symptoms: A prospective population-based cohort study, *Journal of Affective Disorders*, 2021.

249 C. Deforges, S. Stuijfzand, Y. Noël, M. Robertson, T. Breines Simonsen, M. Eberhard-Gran, S. Garthus-Niegel, A. Horsch, The rela- tionship between early administration of morphine or nitrous oxide gas and PTSD symptom development, *Journal of Affective Disorders*, 2021.

250 S. Stuijfzand, S. Garthus-Niegel, A. Horsch, Parental birth- related PTSD symptoms and bonding in the early postpartum period: A prospective population-based cohort study, *Frontiers in Psychiatry*, 2020.

251 S. Garthus-Niegel, A. Horsch, S. Ayers, J. Junge-Hoffmeister, K. Weidner, M. Eberhard-Gran, The influence of postpartum PTSD on breastfeeding: A long-itudinal population-based study, *Birth*, 2018.

252 www.midwiferytoday.com/mt-articles/ptsd-and-obstetric-violence/

253 E. L. Moses-Kolko *et al.*, In search of neural endopheno- types of postpartum psychopathology and disrupted maternal caregiving, *Journal of Neuroendocrinoly*, 2014.

254 D. S. Schechter *et al.*, An fMRI study of the brain responses of traumatized mothers to viewing their toddlers during separation and play, *Social Cognitive and Affective Neuroscience*, 2012.

255 E. L. Moses-Kolko *et al.*, In search of neural endophenotypes of postpartum psychopathology and disrupted maternal caregiving, art. cit.

256 S. Kim *et al.*, Mothers' unresolved trauma blunts amygdala response to infant distress, *Social Neuroscience*, 2017.

257 P. Kim, C. G. Capistrano, A. Erhart, R. Gray-Schiff, N. Xu, Socioeconomic disadvantage, neural responses to infant emotions, and emotional availability among first-time new mothers, *Behavioural Brain Research*, 2017.

258 J. Levy, K. Yirmiya, A. Goldstein, R. Feldman, The neural basis of empathy and empathic behavior in the context of chronic trauma, *Frontiers in Psychiatry*, 2019.

259 A. Horsch *et al.*, Reducing intrusive traumatic memories after emergency caesarean section: A proof-of-principle randomized controlled study, *Behaviour Research and Therapy*, 2017.

260 Tears are classified into four grades. The second degree tear affects the vagina and the perineum (set of muscles between the anus and the vagina).

261 M. Willets, What it means to be a rainbow baby and why rainbow babies are beautiful, www.parents.com, 2018.

262 A. Serfaty, Stillbirth in France, *The Lancet*, 2014.

263 C. Burden *et al.*, From grief, guilt pain and stigma to hope and pride—a systematic review and meta-analysis of mixed-method research of the psychosocial impact of stillbirth, *BMC Pregnancy and Childbirth*, 2016.

264 A. K. Lewkowitz *et al.*, Association between stillbirth ≥ 23 weeks gestation and acute psychiatric illness within 1 year of delivery, *American Journal of Obstetrics and Gynecology*, 2019.

265 J. Farren *et al.*, Post-traumatic stress, anxiety and depression following miscarriage and ectopic pregnancy: a multi-center, prospective, cohort study, *American Journal of Obstetrics and Gynecology*, 2020.

266 L. Demarchi, J.L. Pawluski, O.J. Bosch. The brain oxytocin and corticotropin-releasing factor systems in grieving mothers: What we know and what we need to learn. *Peptides*. 2021 Sep;143:170593.

267 J. L. Pawluski, B. L. Vanderbyl, K. Ragan, L. A. Galea, First reproductive experience persistently affects spatial reference and working memory in the mother and these effects are not due to pregnancy or "mothering" alone, art. cit.

268 J.L Pawluski, S.E. Lieblich, L.A. Galea. Offspring-exposure reduces depressive-like behaviour in the parturient female rat. *Behav Brain Res*, 2009, Jan 30;197(1): 55-61.

269 https://www.jodipawluski.com/mommybrainrevisited/episode/2192b74c /12-partner-loss-and-the-maternal-brain

270 L. Demarchi, J.L. Pawluski, O.J. Bosch. The brain oxytocin and corticotropin-releasing factor systems in grieving mothers: What we know and what we need to learn. *Peptides*. 2021 Sep;143:170593.

271 R. Orso *et al.*, Maternal behavior of the mouse dam toward pups: implications for maternal separation model of early life stress, *Stress*, 2018.

272 E. Yong. "What a Grieving Orca Tells Us". *The Atlantic*. August 14, 2018.

273 E. Lesser. *Cassandra Speaks. When Women Are the Storytellers, the Human Story Changes*. Harper Wave, 2020.

274 www.youtube.com/watch?v=uihF7_oLgo4

275 www.youtube.com/watch?v=-MUauB2HpYA, *"All you want to know about Daddy Blues"*

276 www.nytimes.com/2021/07/19/well/mind/men-postpartum-depression.html

277 D. B. Singley, L. M. Edwards, Men's perinatal mental health in the transition to fatherhood, *Professional Psychology. Research and Practice*, 2015. J.F. Paulson *et al.*, Individual and combined effects of postpartum depression in mothers and fathers on parenting behavior, *Pediatrics*, 2006.

278 P. Kim, J. E. Swain, Sad dads: paternal postpartum depression, *Psychiatry*, 2007.

279 N. Fairbrother *et al.*, Prepartum and postpartum mothers' and fathers' unwanted, intrusive thoughts in response to infant crying, *Behavioural and Cognitive Psychotherapy*, 2019.

280 J. A. Leiferman *et al.*, Anxiety among fathers during the prenatal and post-partum period: a meta-analysis, *Journal of Psychosomatic Obstetrics & Gynecology*, 2021.

281 S. D. Fisher, Paternal mental health: Why is it relevant?, *American Journal of Lifestyle Medicine*, 2016.

282 J. L. Pawluski, Perinatal selective serotonin reuptake inhibitor exposure: impact on brain development and neural plasticity, *Neuroendocrinology*, 2012. M. Gemmel *et al.*, Perinatal selective serotonin reuptake inhibitor medication (SSRI) effects on social behaviors, neurodevelopment and the epigenome, *Neuroscience & Biobehavioral Reviews*, 2018.

283  8th World Congress on Women's Mental Health, March 2019, Paris.

284  A.-S. Rommel *et al.*, Long-term prenatal effects of antidepressant use on the risk of affective disorders in the offspring: A register-based cohort study, *Neuropsychopharmacology*, 2021.

285  P. Kim *et al.*, Neural plasticity in fathers of human infants, art. cit.

286  D. E. Saxbe *et al.*, High paternal testosterone may protect against postpartum depressive symptoms in fathers, but confer risk to mothers and children, *Hormones and Behavior*, 2017.

287  A. Isacco *et al.*, An examination of fathers' mental health help seeking: A brief report, *American Journal of Men's Health*, 2015.

288  K. Kleiman *The Art of Holding in Therapy*. Routledge, 2017.

289  J. L. Pawluski, M. Li, J. S. Lonstein, Serotonin and motherhood: From molecules to mood, *Frontiers in Neuroendocrinology*, 2019.

290  J. E. Swain et al., Parent-child intervention decreases stress and increases maternal brain activity and connectivity during own baby-cry: An exploratory study, *Development and Psychopathology*, 2017.

291  https://medicine.umich.edu/dept/psychiatry/programs/zero-thrive/clinical-service/mom-power

292  M. Muzik *et al.*, Mom power: Preliminary outcomes of a group intervention to improve mental health and parenting among high-risk mothers, *Archives of Women's Mental Health*, 2015. M. Muzik *et al.*, A mental health and parenting intervention for adolescent and young adult mothers and their infants, *Journal of Depression and Anxiety*, 2016.

293  Swain JE, *et al.* Parent-child intervention decreases stress and increases maternal brain activity and connectivity during own baby-cry: An exploratory study. *Dev Psychopathol*, 2017.

294  www.instagram.com/postpartum_tamere/

295  www.instagram.com/p/CaD5pl9J2mT

296  C. Bondar, *Wild Moms. Motherhood in the Animal Kingdom*. Pegasus Books, 2018.

Deepest appreciation to
Demeter's monthly Donors

**DEMETER**

**Daughters**
Tatjana Takseva
Debbie Byrd
Fiona Green
Tanya Cassidy
Vicki Noble
Myrel Chernick

**Sisters**
Amber Kinser
Nicole Willey

**Grandmother**
Tina Powell